Power From Above:
A Memoir

James Adams

POWER FROM ABOVE

Copyright © 2014 by James Adams

All rights reserved. No part of this book may be reproduced or transmitted in any form or by any means without written permission of the author.

Sketches by Christin Adams

Photographer by Andrew Johnson

Edited by Mary McBeth, www.UrbanFictionEditor.com
Layout and Interior Design by: UrbanFictionMedia.com

ISBN 978-0-692-31011-3

To my mother Sylvia,
wife Lena,
daughter Christin,
and son James
with love eternal

Acknowledgments

Much love and thanks to:

My mother Sylvia for all the love and support,

My wife Lena, daughter Christin and son James, who mean the world to me, and gives me the strength to rise each day,

My brothers Gilbert, Jason, John and sisters Sharon and Leslie, for all the love and encouragement over the years,

My father James, for help bringing me into this world,

My maternal and paternal grandparents, who are looking down from the heavens,

My cousins, aunts, uncles, nieces, nephews and in-laws for all the love,

My cousins Carl, Debbie, Courtney, and Carl Walker Jr. for welcoming me into their home and inspiring me to achieve and be a family man,

My Kappa Alpha Psi fraternity brothers,

My homies- living and deceased,

Dr. Richard Wertime- for your teachings and guidance through the Masters program, which helped inspire me to write this book,

My high school and college basketball team mates,

My editor Mary McBeth and her team, for your keen editorial skills and creativity,

All the victims of domestic violence who I hope are inspired by this book,

And most of all to God- with him,
all things are possible.

Table of Contents

PROLOGUE 1
Chapter 1: Near Death Experience 3
Chapter 2: Domestic Violence 7
Chapter 3: My Biological 17
Chapter 4: Mt. Airy Groove...23
Chapter 5: The Uptown 29
Chapter 6: Marijuana: The Drug of Choice 35
Chapter 7: My New Hood..39
Chapter 8: Basketball Saved My Life.........................47
Chapter 9: Highschool Days..55
Chapter 10: Playing With The Pros 67
Chapter 11: BBall: College Style 77
Chapter 12: Meeting My Soulmate..............................83
Chapter 13: Joining The Frat 91
Chapter 14: Crack..99
Chapter 15: With God, All Things Are Possible 103

PROLOGUE

I came into this world during the height of the civil rights movement in the 1960s. In 1962, James Meredith became a hero in the African American community as the first African American student to enroll at the University of Mississippi. He stood up for his rights despite all of the harassment he received from White protestors, his fellow students and national newsmakers. In May 1963, seven months after James Meredith became the first African-American student at the University of Mississippi, I was born and given my father's first name, James. Since James Meredith's heroic stand was still a hot topic at that time, my godmother gave me my middle name—Meredith.

Meanwhile, the civil rights movement was picking up steam. During the civil rights protests in Birmingham, Alabama, fire hoses and dogs were used on Black demonstrators. These images were televised and helped to gain sympathy for the civil rights movement around the world.

I was five months old when Dr. Martin Luther King made his famous "I Have a Dream" speech. When I look back on the footage from those days, I am very touched by the fact that Dr. Martin Luther King and others dedicated their lives to make America a better place for me and my family. That's why I've always had nothing but love for my fellow Americans, no matter the color of one's skin. To hate others is counterproductive to what Dr. King and others have done for our country.

I was born in Philadelphia, Pennsylvania. Like other American cities at the time, Philadelphia, the City of Brotherly Love, experienced racial tension between Whites and Blacks. Under Frank Rizzo's leadership, police were known for horrific brutality against Blacks. In the Black community, the police were called derisive terms like, "Pigs", or "The Man", which implied that the police represented the powerful White man and were trying to keep Blacks down. In 1964, as I took my first steps, North Philadelphia erupted in devastating race riots due to allegations of police brutality. Many Blacks were injured and arrested. Ironically, three years later, two White police officers rushed to a small North Philadelphia street for a different reason, to save the life of a four year old Black boy. That street was Bancroft street and that little boy was me.

Chapter 1:
Near Death Experience

Like many North Philadelphia streets, Bancroft Street is a long narrow street, only two cars wide. So when cars are parked on either side of it, there is barely enough room for a car to drive down the block. Bancroft Street is lined with about 50 small row houses on each side. Bancroft Street was two blocks away from Firth Street, which was the street where I lived. On several occasions, I would visit my Aunt Emma, who lived on Bancroft Street. I loved visiting Aunt Emma, especially since there were more kids to play with on her block. In the summer of 1967, Bancroft Street was filled with kids playing hopscotch, tag, jump rope, wall ball and other games. I remember sitting on the outside house steps getting my hair platted and eating cake the girls made with their toy cake ovens. In those days, each North Philadelphia street was like a small village. Everyone looked out for each other.

One day, I was staying over my Aunt Emma's house on Bancroft Street. I was playing wall ball with a few of the boys who lived on the block when I heard the musical siren of the ice cream truck as it slowly rolled down the narrow street. Someone exclaimed, "The ice cream man is coming!" and most of the kids, including myself, hurried to the truck like mice following the Pied Piper.

As I was running toward the truck, a car turned the corner doing 60 miles per hour down the narrow street. A loud thump was heard by the surrounding kids. Witnesses say my body flew six feet in the air as the car crashed into my tiny four-year-old frame. When I hit the concrete pavement, my head hit the ground first and I was knocked unconscious with blood pouring from a gash in my head. Other kids stood by and were in shock as they looked on at my unconscious face, smashed in a pool of blood. They must have thought I was dead.

My Aunt Emma heard the screeching car tires and the loud thump from her living room. She rushed out of her house and saw my still body lying on the ground.

She screamed, "Oh my God, it's Joey!" Joey was the nickname given to me by my older brother, Jack, who was a fan of the Joey Bishop show, which aired on one of the few TV channels that existed back then in the 1960s.

Power From Above

My Aunt Emma told me later that she ran back into her house to call for help. After calling 911, my aunt immediately called my Mom.

Mom answered the phone, "Hello?"

My aunt responded in a distraught voice, "Joey was just hit by a car." My mother screamed and started crying; she later told me her normally caramel-colored face grew pale as the life seemed to drain out of her as she heard the news.

"I think he's still alive; I just called 911. They're on the way," my aunt said.

"Oh no, my baby! I'll be right there," my mom dropped the phone. She quickly grabbed her purse and rushed out of the house as tears ran down her face. We lived on Firth Street, a few blocks away from Bancroft Street.

Before my mom arrived, two police officers rushed to my aid. They grabbed me from the ground, placed me in the police car and rushed me to the hospital. When my mother arrived at Bancroft street, I was already gone. There were a few additional police cars that responded to the 911 call. Two police officers in one of the cars drove my mom to the hospital.

Throughout my life, I kept remembering my ride to the hospital in that police car. I remember hovering over my body, looking down from the ceiling of the car as one of the police officers performed CPR. I was only four years old, but the image and memory of the event is still very vivid. As I got older and did more research, I discovered that my experience was called a near-death experience.

James Adams

Like others who have had near-death experiences, I felt no pain as I hovered over my body. I do not recall going through a tunnel or into the light, but I visited a place where I was circled by several beings. I felt protected. I felt pure love. I just remember they promised to watch over me and protect me. I don't know who they were, because I was too young to know any relatives that had passed prior to the event. Were they angels? Spirits of my ancestors? I guess that's why I've always felt like I'm being watched, even when I'm alone.

The next thing I remembered, back in my body, I was awake and being fed at the hospital. I finally recovered, but it's a miracle that I survived. I could easily have died that day. It took around 15 billion years for me to come into existence, and it took only four years to almost lose my life on earth. I owe a great deal to those two cops who rushed to Bancroft Street to save the life of a small little boy, and although I credit them for saving my life, a higher power was at work that day. God planted a seed of faith, and now it only needed to be nourished and grow. It was not my destiny to die that day.

Surviving the car accident was just one of many miracles I've experienced throughout my life. I was and still am a witness to the power and blessings I have received from above.

Chapter 2:
Domestic Violence

It's no secret that America was built on a foundation of violence. Throughout history, violence has been used to gain power, land and money. The 1960s saw the climax of more than three hundred years of violent exchanges when, for the first time, Blacks across the country became fed up, organized, worked together and fought to gain their civil rights. The great Martin Luther King, Jr. fought to end the violence through the use of nonviolence. Although violence and intimidation were major ways the American Whites used to gain power and control over Black people, Dr. King felt that Blacks would gain the power they sought with nonviolent protests.

Unfortunately, it was a violent act that killed Dr. King in 1968, when I was four years old. Seven days later, President Johnson signed the Civil Rights Act of 1968, prohibiting discrimination in the sale, rental, and financing of housing. The Civil Rights Act of 1964 had already made it a crime to discriminate for any other reason, Dr. King was working nonviolently to help Blacks utilize the rights they had already been given on paper, but not in practice, hence the reason Mr. James Meredith, although given the legal right two years earlier, had such obstacles attending the

University of Mississippi in 1962. This means it was legal, but police would not help us in the South when Whites refused to honor these rights.

Dr. King's life work made a huge impact in making America a better place to live for Blacks and the human race in general. Through his peaceful protests, he made it possible for Blacks to eat anywhere we wished and sit anywhere we wanted to on public transportation as well as attend whatever school we wanted to.

Ironically, the violence I was exposed to at a young age didn't involve Whites at all. I've never fought a White person, nor had I ever been threatened by a White person. The violence I witnessed growing up involved Blacks beating up or killing other Blacks——"Black on Black violence." Growing up, I had to deal with gang violence in the streets and violence in the home.

In the 1960s through the early 1970s, Philadelphia had one of the highest gang-related homicide rates in the country. I lived close to gangs like 15th and Venango and 25th and Diamond. Another big gang in Philly was PGH (Pimps, Gangsters and Hustlers). Back then, many of the gangs used fists and knives to resolve disputes. But as guns increased in the hoods, so did the murder rate.

One of the biggest gang fights I've witnessed happened after a house party near Broad and Erie. Members of several gangs attended the party, which was a recipe for disaster. I was sitting on my front steps and saw the gangs assemble in front of a house, which was 10 doors from my house. As I watched the crowd grow, a full out brawl erupted between several people within the crowd. I ran into the house and told my mom to look out the front window. The next thing I heard was my mom shouting, "Joey, lie on the floor!" As she turned out the lights, the guns started firing. Cop cars flooded the neighborhood. The police got out of their cars with guns out, firing more gunshots into the air—bang, bang, bang——in an effort to control the crowd of gang members. It was a scene right out of the movies, but that was real life in the 'hood. The police finally gained control and made arrests. The street was back to normal until the next gang war.

In those days, living in the 'hood was tough. I was always big for my age, so when I was six or seven, I didn't fight other six- or seven-year-olds; I had to fight teenagers. I used to hate 3:00 p.m., because that's when all the schools let out, and I usually got into a fight before I made it home. It wasn't like I started these fights. Some kids just seemed to be full of hate and wanted to act out their frustrations through fighting. It seemed like Dr. King's message of nonviolence wasn't getting through to the urban neighborhood.

One day, I was jumped by two older kids hanging on a nearby corner, one block from where I lived. Why they jumped me, I do not know. One of the big kids asked me, "What are you doing around here?" The next thing I knew, he was punching on me, and the other kid joined in. All I could do was get against a wall and try to cover up. "We're going to kick your ass!" Again, why? I do not know and they never told me. My guess is that it was a territorial thing; that was one of the mentalities of the gangs back in the sixties, which were mostly made up of older teens and young men, and it transferred to the younger teenagers. If you walked on their territory, which could have been any neighborhood block or corner, you were open game.

My older brother Jack found out I was jumped by two teenagers and he was furious. He didn't live with me at the time, he was nine years older than I and lived in New Jersey with his father. But he always had my back. He took me around the corner to where I was jumped to look for the boys. We couldn't find them, but he had no problem walking up to a corner of gang members and introducing himself.

He said, "Hey, this is my little brother and I'm looking for the two guys who jumped him." Of course, they didn't know anything. Jack told them, "I'm from Jersey, but I'll be back if anything else happens to my little brother. Do me a favor and keep an eye out for him."

That exchange went better than I'd expected. The guys on the corner could tell my brother wasn't afraid of them. My brother was big and very intimidating himself. Although I still got into fights, I had no more problems from anyone on that particular street corner.

The violence I saw and had to deal with on the streets, was nothing compared to the violence I witnessed in my own home. In the 1960s the women, who were getting their asses kicked by their husbands, unfortunately felt trapped in their relationships. During this time, most men were the sole source of their family's income. Women were reluctant to leave their abusers, because the women didn't have jobs, or made very little income. Some made a little side money doing ironing or taking care of others' kids, but most women had no other place to go, because there weren't many domestic violence shelters in the sixties.

Women were also discouraged from reporting the violence in the home, because most domestic violence cases weren't treated in the criminal courts. They were considered "family problems" and handled in the family court. A man could get into more trouble assaulting a stranger than he would assaulting his wife. When police were called to break up domestic disputes, they would maybe hold the husband for a night, if he was drunk or uncontrollably irate, but then the husband would be back home the next day, eventually kicking his wife's ass again. It was a vicious cycle.

The horror in our home began when I was five years old. At the time, my mother and I were living alone on Firth Street in North Philly, as one of my older brothers lived in New Jersey with his father, the other was in the military, and my sister got married and moved out. My dad? Well, we'll get to him later on. Anyway, my mother's friend, Emma, wanted my then 40-year-old divorced single mom to meet her brother, Josh. My mom and Josh eventually met and went out to dinner. After a period of dating, they eventually purchased a house together on Broad and Erie and we settled into our new home. Josh was a butcher, so he made a good salary and would treat my mom to some of the finest cuts of meats. Josh and my mom eventually married and my mom became pregnant. In 1968, my little brother, Jay, was born. I was excited about the new additions to the family—my brother Jay, and my stepfather, Josh.

James Adams

I liked Josh. When my mom and he were dating, he would get on the floor and play race cars with me. I was young, so it was easy to win me over with a little playtime. Other than my brother's father Bill, Josh was the only father figure I knew at the time. Although I was happy to have a father figure around, my mother and I soon discovered that we were living with Dr. Jekyll and Mr. Hyde. Josh was one of the nicest guys ever when he was sober, but after he drank his powerful potion, he turned into an evil monster. I remember one of his elixirs of choice—Ballantine beer. I can still picture the bottles with the three ring logo turning upside down as he chugged it.

Each night as he began his drinking, my heart used to drop into my gut because I knew what was next. After their honeymoon period ended, the arguing between Josh and my mother increased dramatically. The arguing always happened after Josh was drinking. I could have lived with just arguing, but the arguing soon turned to violence.

The tiniest thing would set him off. My mom became his personal punching bag. As a five year old kid, I was traumatized seeing my mom get pummeled by Josh. My mom wasn't a tiny woman, but when Josh started beating on her, he would throw her around like a rag doll. I can still visualize her being thrown around the room and repeatedly punched in the face as she screamed, "Josh, please stop! Please ... please." All my mom could do was cry and scream and plead for her life.

This wasn't the type of violence you see on television. This violence was live in living color. And watching your mom get beat up is one of the most horrendous acts one can witness. Many times she was beat to near death. Her beautiful caramel- colored face turned bloody and swollen from the violent blows.

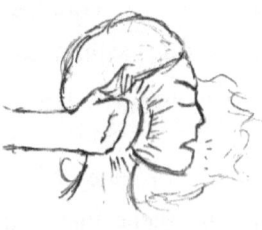

As a five-year-old, all I could do was call the police. I used to call the police like it was my job. The police would come and save my mom's life every time. They would hold Josh in a cell overnight. Once he was sober the next day, he would apologize and all would be well until the next drink. I always used to know when my mom was headed for another beat down. He would get drunk and start raising his voice. My heart would drop, because I knew what was coming. My mom would receive another beating, I'd call the police and they'd hold Josh for the night. The next morning, Josh asked for forgiveness. "Please forgive me Queenie, you know I love you and will never hit you again." Josh would always call my mom Queenie.

Queenie would always forgive Josh, but she didn't forget. She showed me a stash of money she used to hide under the rug in my baby brother's room. "Look Joey, here's the money I'm saving. Soon I will have enough money to leave Josh." We would finally be free from his reign of terror. I recalled my near-death experience and that feeling of being watched from above, and I prayed to that watcher. Although it was tough seeing my mom get her frequent beat downs, I knew that my prayers were being heard and that one day, this hell we were living in would cease.

Unfortunately, before we could escape Josh's horrific sway over our household, I witnessed the worst assault on my mom to date. I can still hear the screams of pain as my mom rolled around the floor, and was thrown into furniture, just helpless against the barrage of punches to her face and body. It was a graphic scene that is hard for me to think about, because it was a living nightmare.

I called the police again and Josh was held for a few days. The police planned to hold Josh long enough to give us a chance to move out. We stayed at my Aunt Gloria's house for a few days as the swelling and black and blue bruises from my mom's face healed. While staying there, my cousin Jimmy stopped over and was shocked to see my mom's swollen, black and blue face.

"Who did that to you!" he demanded to know. My mom couldn't even say Josh's name.

My aunt shouted, "Josh did it to her!" Jimmy was furious. He and my brother were ready to kick Josh's ass.

Instead of moving out of the house, my mom decided to forgive Josh again. We left my aunt's house and went back home. I knew it wouldn't be long before the violence happened again. When it did, this time I called my brother Jack and cousin Jimmy. They came in the house and without one word, just started beating Josh's ass. The first punch knocked Josh into the fish tank-it fell over and exploded.

There were fish flapping all over the floor. Then, Jimmy pinned Josh down on the couch and must have punched him in the face fifty times.

"If you ever hit my aunt again, I'll be back to kick your ass again." It was a beautiful sight. Josh was the one getting beat up instead of my mom. He was helpless with each punch to his face. The shoe was now on the other foot.

Josh's beat down seem to calm him down for a while, but he probably didn't remember much of it, because he was drunk. It would only take until the next time he drank; he would then go after my mom again. The last straw finally came.

One evening, on his way home from work, Josh made a stop at the bar and had a few drinks. He came home smashed. It didn't take long before he and my mom got into an argument.

"Where's my fucking dinner?" he barked.

"You were late, I put the food away," my mom responded. But Josh wasn't happy with that answer at all.

"I don't give a fuck if I was late or not, my dinner should be hot and waiting for me!" It didn't matter what my mom said or did; when Josh was drunk, she was in a no-win situation.

Like previous times, I was poised by the phone, because I knew what was coming. But this time was different. Josh did something he never did before—he pulled out a butcher knife and went after my mom. A butcher knife in a drunken butcher's hand is never a good idea, especially when that drunk was Josh. My mom also did something she never did before—she didn't hesitate to grab me and my little brother and rush out of the house. Josh pulling out that butcher knife was the "straw that broke the camel's back."

We escaped and ran down to the intersection of Broad and Erie, she in her robe and me and Jay in our pajamas. Everyone in the neighborhood probably knew what evil we were escaping that evening. But God and his angels were protecting us. My mom ran into a phone booth on the corner and called one of her best friends who lived in Mount Airy.

"Stacey, Josh got drunk again and grabbed a butcher knife. He chased Joey and me out of the house. We're at Broad and Erie and need a place to stay." We jumped in a cab and went to Ms. Stacey's house in Mount Airy, which was several miles away.

I would never see Josh again. God answered my prayers.

Chapter 3:
My Biological

According to the U.S. Census Bureau, approximately 24 million children in America live in biological father-absent homes. Consequently, having the biological father absent in many homes has a negative effect on many of the social issues facing America—poverty, emotional/behavioral problems, incarceration, crime, child and woman abuse, education, drugs and more. Unfortunately, I was one of the 24 million children that had to grow up without his biological father in the home.

A man approached a small row house in North Philadelphia. He knocked on the door.

"Mom, someone is at the door."

"Okay, I'll get it." My mom opened the door. The man had on a military uniform. He came into the house and took off his hat to reveal a small afro. In the other hand, he was carrying a big bag of Chinese food.

"Hey son," he said as he patted my head. He kissed my mom and placed the food on the table. "I've brought dinner."

James Adams

That was the earliest image I remember of my father, who was a Master Sergeant in the United States Army. My dad's nickname was "The Bull," because he had a big, stocky six foot body frame. He and my mom dated a few times in the early 1960s. They were introduced by my Dad's sister, Aunt Beth. Aunt Beth and my mom were good friends—they would go out on double dates together. One night, my mom and dad got very intimate, and I was the product of a "booty call."

My dad married his main girl, Helen, while he was stationed in Hawaii. He had been dating her since the 1950s, well before I was born. About once a year, my dad would fly to Philly to visit his family and friends, and I even got a chance to see him.

My dad and I were never really that close. He was my father, but we didn't have a close father and son relationship. I did have a great relationship with his mother, sisters, brothers and my cousins. I would visit them pretty often. Especially my grandmother, who I loved to death. She was a great strong-spirited woman who everyone loved. She was respected by her family, neighborhood and church. She thought about me often and made me "sock it to me" cakes for my birthday, which she knew were my favorite.

My grandmother lived in a big three story house in North Philly. Several of my aunts, uncles and cousins lived there with her. She was not only the matriarch of the family, but she was also the matriarch of her neighborhood. Her block would often take bus trips to the Hershey and Dorney amusement parks. I can still taste the fried chicken my grandmother made for the bus trips. I loved my grandmother dearly and she wanted to make sure my father and I stayed connected.

When I was eight years old, I recall playing outside while anxiously waiting for my father to come pick me up for a visit. He pulled up in his rental car and got out, "Hi son, get your things. You're staying over your Aunt Beth's house for a few days." When I wasn't visiting my Grandmother, I loved staying at my aunt's house, because I got a chance to play with my cousin, Will, who was a year younger than I.

During times when my father was home in Hawaii, my aunt would always get on me about writing my father.

"Did you write your father? I know he'd like to hear from you."

"No, I haven't written him in a while, but I will."

"Okay, here's his address and phone number in case you lost it."

"Thanks, Auntie." Whenever my aunt gave me my dad's address, it didn't match the PO Box address he told me to send letters to—the address my aunt gave me was an actual street address. And he never gave me his phone number, he would always call me.

When I was a younger, I never gave much thought about why I was sending letters to my dad via a PO Box. I never wondered why he never gave his home address. Why did my aunt send letters to his home address, and I had to send letters to a PO Box? One day, I decided to go ahead a write him a letter to his home address.

During that time, one of my older cousins named John, was visiting with my father in Hawaii. Although I was his son, my cousins had a closer relationship with my father than I did. That always bothered me. I didn't care that my cousins had a strong relationship with my father, that was great, but it bothered me that I didn't have a strong relationship with him. My dad invited a few of my cousins to stay with him in Hawaii, but I've never been there yet. John stayed about eight years in Hawaii and was probably more like a son to my father than I. I liked John; he actually had my back.

When my letter arrived at my father's house, all hell broke loose. My father's wife opened my letter and took it to my father. "What's this?" She handed the letter to my father. He read it while my cousin looked over my father's shoulder.

"That's my cousin Joey," John said proudly, "your stepson."

I don't know the rest of the conversation, because my cousin John told me he was asked to leave the room so they could continue their discussion. I guess the cat was out of the bag. My dad had to finally tell his wife that he had a son she knew nothing about.

Within the first six years of my life, I had a near-death experience and had to deal with the horrors of violence in my neighborhood and inside my own house. While I was dealing with an abusive stepfather, where was my biological father when I needed him the most? He was hundreds of miles away. I prayed to God that when I had kids, I would be in their lives each and every day.

Chapter 4:
Mt. Airy Groove

In 1971, Marvin Gaye released his popular album, "What's Going On." The album focused on the view of a Vietnam War vet returning home, only to see suffering from drugs and poverty, injustice and hatred. Through music, Marvin Gaye made people think about the many evils that plagued the world at that time. It was during this time that I not only learned more about the good Lord, but I also knew he was a part of me.

After moving to Mount Airy in '71, I met another boy who had experienced a bad domestic violence situation. George was older than I was, so he wasn't a helpless little boy witnessing his mom get beat down; he was old enough to take action. One night, his actions resulted in the fatal shooting of his father. Even if I was older and had access to a gun, I don't think I could have taken Josh's life. But given the chance that night, would I have taken Josh the butcher's life to save my mom's life?

George was faced with that decision and chose to save his Mom's life. It was an action George paid the price for by serving time in the Youth Study Center, a prison for teenagers. He once told me the memory of killing his father was something he had to deal with for the rest of his life. But, while in prison, George became close to someone powerful—someone powerful enough to ease his pain during lockup, and powerful enough to forgive him for murdering his father. That someone was the all- powerful Lord Jesus Christ.

George and I spent many nights reading the Bible. He would read out loud, "For God so loved the world that he gave his one and only Son, that whoever believes in him shall not perish but have eternal life." As we read the Bible, I would get this overwhelming feeling of love. The message gave me an inner strength and connection to God.

George would break down and explain many of the passages to me. Although I had the near-death experience and felt that some good spirits were watching over me, I began to have a deeper understanding of my relationship with the Lord. That seed God planted several years prior was starting to be nourished. As I learned about the Lord and God our Father, that feeling of love continued to grow, and my heart felt full of pure love. My spirit was touched by the Lord.

During this time in my life, I not only strengthened my relationship with the Lord Jesus Christ, but I was having big fun in Mount Airy. The grip of fear Josh held over our family was gone. We were able to move on, make new friends and take advantage of new opportunities.

My Mom's friend, Stacey, had three sons, Bobby, Bill and Paul. Paul was closer to my age, so we hung out and played a lot. Bobby had a paper route. Paul and I would go out with him to help with the paper route. Eventually, Bobby hooked me up with my own paper route. I had to get

Power From Above

up at 5:00 a.m. to start delivering papers each day. I was only eight years old, but it was fun having a paper route. I always kept money in my pocket when I went out to collect the weekly balance owed for the papers.

Back then, when you had $5 to $10 in your pocket, you were the man. I remember treating all of the kids to ice cream from the Good Humor truck. Looking back on that time, having money wasn't always a good thing. It was during this time that I was introduced to weed.

When I was eight years old, I was big enough to pass for 12 to 13 years old. I rolled with an older crowd for the most part. They were mostly teenagers around 14 to 17 years old, some maybe older. They, along with my older siblings, turned me on to weed. Having money allowed me to be able to chip in for "nickel bags" of the stuff and at five dollars a bag, we stayed high pretty often. When most eight-year-olds were thinking about school and playing kid games, I was thinking about weed and girls. I remember sitting in my 4th grade classroom, high as a kite.

"Joey, are you okay?" the teacher would ask. I guess she thought my eyes were red due to a cold, but I was high, just chilling out. I was a very smart student, but when you're high, you don't function in class very well. When you're an eight-year-old, the only thing attractive about getting high is you feel cool, because you're doing something the older kids are doing. I didn't enjoy the feeling of paranoia, but I did find it interesting to trip over certain situations that wouldn't ordinarily seem so deep. Things like normal interactions with people, or just self-awareness and the feeling of being enlightened.

I lived in a four unit apartment building that had two apartments on each floor. I lived upstairs in an apartment across from the owner. The owner had a son named Bean. Bean was one of the older kids who turned me on to weed and older women. Bean was "the man." He used to have parties in our basement, red light and all. We used to turn on the slow music like, "Lay Lady, Lay" from the Isley Brothers, and let the slow dancing begin. It was common to see us grinding on girls against the wall or against the washer and dryer. When I used to have my birthday parties, the kids from my school thought they were the best and looked forward to them. I used to hear people say, "Joey throws some of the best parties, they're not little kiddy parties." I was a young kid starting to live in the fast lane.

One evening, Bean had the apartment to himself and invited this fine "redbone" to come over his place. Of course he invited his boys over too. A girl with a nice Afro came in the apartment wearing tight blue jeans, which highlighted her booty. Supposedly, she was willing to have sex with all of us, so we were going to pull a train on her. It was the seventies and sex and smoking weed were popular things to do when teenagers got together. I had no father in my life at the time, so the older teenagers were my role models. I thought sex and smoking weed were normal things to do.

Bean took the girl into his bedroom, and started having sex with her. After a while, I remember one of the older kids named Lee started banging on Bean's bedroom door, because he was supposed to be next. "Yo, Bean, what's taking so long, I'm next man, open the door." Needless to say, she only had sex with Bean that night, regardless how much we all pounded on the bedroom door. Not saying I would have done anything; I wasn't even 10 years old yet, just trying to hang with the big boys.

Bean wasn't the only guy in the neighborhood with the girls. I myself connected with a neighborhood honey named Sarah. Sarah was a few years older than I, but loved to hook up with me. One day I took her to the Uptown to see Shaft. In one scene, my man Shaft was having sex with his woman. Sarah leaned over and whispered in my ear, "Do you want to go home and do what they're doing?"

I said, "Hell yeah!" That day and several more days, we would turn on the slow music in the basement and just lie on top of each other and grind. It wasn't the real thing, but it felt good as we were grinding to the Chi-lites' singing, "Oh, girl, I'd be in trouble if you left me now, cause I don't know where to look for love, I just don't know how ..."

Sarah was the first girl who made me feel jealous and act territorial in a relationship. One day I heard the music playing in the basement. The basement was shared by the four apartments, but anyone had access if they walked into the apartment building. I went down to investigate, and to my surprise, my boy Paul was grinding on top of Sarah.

"Yo, what are you two doing?" I asked. But I knew. They looked at me and quickly got up.

Sarah said to me, "Sorry Joey, it just happened." I knew she was the one who asked Paul to grind on her, as we did previously.

I felt betrayed. That feeling of being cheated on is a horrible feeling. It digs deep into your emotions and you feel like crap. That was my first lesson in having a relationship. It was something I had to experience so I knew what to avoid in the future. God was letting me know that if you want to play with fire, you will get burnt. Lesson learned.

Chapter 5:
The Uptown

The Uptown Theater opened in 1929 on Broad Street. It featured a lavish art deco interior. The building was then owned by Sam Stiefel. In the 1960s, it was purchased by the Milgram family who owned many of the theaters in the Philadelphia area. During that time, the Uptown Theater became an historic mecca of rhythm and blues and comedy known across the United States. The Uptown Theater hosted many famous acts that included Ray Charles, James Brown, Jackie Wilson, Stevie Wonder, the Isley Brothers, Marvin Gaye, BB King, Martha Reeves, The Supremes, the Jackson Five and many more. In the early 1970s, I practically lived at the Uptown. The Uptown was a big influence in my life for many reasons.

In October 1969, to my great delight, my older sister, Ann, was hired as the cashier at The Uptown. Ann became friends with many of the singers that performed at The Uptown; she hung out with Cool and the Gang, The Moments, The Manhattans, The Persuaders, The Spinners, The Blue Moments, The O'Jays and The Stylistics. She eventually dated one of the singers from the Stylistics, whose nickname is Junie. Ann would take me backstage to meet many of the singers—it was surreal.

James Adams

"Hey Russell, I want you to meet my little brother, Joey. He's a big fan of yours."

"Hi Joey, nice to meet you," Russell said while shaking my hand. Russell was the lead singer of the Stylistics and had a high-pitched voice. One of my favorite songs, "Betcha by Golly, Wow," was a popular song for slow dragging at our basement parties. Now I was meeting the actual person who sang lead on the song.

Eventually, my mom started working at The Uptown too. She had to fill in as the cashier when Ann got pregnant. So basically, I pretty much stayed at the Uptown all day during the summers. When the R & B groups weren't there, I watched movies all day. Black exploitation movies, also known as "Blaxploitation" films, were very popular at the time. Blaxploitation films like Black Caesar, The Mack, Foxy Brown and Super Fly, targeted Black movie goers and featured many of our community's cherished stereotypes in triumphant roles; it was common to see pimps throughout these movies. I loved watching "The Mack" starred Max Julien and Richard Pryor. Max played a pimp named "Goldie." Goldie was released from prison and the movie showed his rise to fame as a big-time pimp. Another movie I loved to watch was "Shaft," which starred Richard Roundtree. Shaft was the man. He was a ladies' man and Black private eye, who kicked butt all over Harlem.

My favorite movies of all were the Bruce Lee movies. I think I saw them all over 100 times each. "The Chinese Connection" and "Fists of Fury" played back to back all day. Bruce Lee, a fearless Kung Fu master, was my hero, because in his movies he would always kick the bullies' asses. I related to this, because there were many bullies in my 'hood that picked on me and others; I wanted to be like Bruce Lee and kick their ass properly. I think everyone would leave Bruce Lee movies practicing kicks and punches; he inspired many to be able to defend themselves. My friend George and I built ourselves each a pair of nunchucks with items purchased from the local hardware store. We would practice using them for several hours each day. I didn't plan to hurt anyone with them, but I felt safer and slightly invincible knowing how to use them.

When I wasn't watching movies, I hung out with Uncle B, or "Unc" as I called him. Unc was the manager of The Uptown. After my mom started working at The Uptown, she and Unc became very close; they had a brother-sister relationship, that's why I considered him my uncle. Unc managed the Uptown with an iron fist. Everyone feared Unc, because he was a no-nonsense type of guy.

While in his office, I told Unc, "My mom said you're a great manager."

"That's right," he responded. "Nothing gets by me. I manage The Uptown from the front door to the back door."

I enjoyed talking with Unc, because he had a relationship with all of the groups that performed at The Uptown; he had a wealth of knowledge and would share many stories with me about some of the Motown R & B acts that were popular at the time.

"Diana Ross asked me to let The Jackson Five perform here, because they needed publicity. You see, once a group like The Jackson Five performs here at the Uptown, the publicity is second to none. Also, once a group makes it here, they end up playing at The Apollo Theater in New York," he told me.

Theaters in Baltimore, Washington, D.C., Philadelphia and New York were a part of the famous Chitlin' Circuit, a string of Black performance venues throughout the East Coast, where it was safe for Black performers to perform back then. If an R & B group performed well at The Uptown Theater, 80 to 90 percent of those groups were able to reach the Apollo Theater, the height of success at that time. The key in the whole circuit was the Uptown—the groups had to perform and do well at The Uptown in order to make it to the Apollo.

"So you played a big part in the success of The Jackson Five?" I asked Unc.

"I would say so," he responded. "They're nice kids, they enjoyed hanging out over Pearl's house. Michael Jackson enjoyed when I took him down the block for ice cream." Pearl lived near The Uptown. Many of the groups enjoyed

Power From Above

hanging out at Pearl's to get home cooked meals. She was like a second mom to them, because many of the groups were away from home for weeks. Hanging out at Pearl's created a family environment for the group members.

Unfortunately, I never got the chance to meet The Jackson Five, but I was happy to be able to meet many of the other R & B groups that performed at The Uptown. Many of the groups, like the Stylistics, were from the Philadelphia area and the Uptown gave them their big chance. For some people, they found success and were able to get out of poverty.

In addition to meeting many of the R & B singers, I enjoyed hanging out with many of the DJ's that hosted shows at The Uptown. Some of the popular DJs that hosted shows at the Uptown were Georgie Woods, Joe "Butterball" Tamburro and Jimmy Bishop. Butterball was a very big Italian American, with a cool voice. He was a DJ at WDAS and became famous for playing Oldies. I loved hanging out with Butterball while my mom was busy in the cashier office. He was always very nice to me.

The radio DJs were very powerful in the 1960s and 70s. The success for an R & B group not only depended on the publicity they received from performing at The Uptown, but also depended on getting their records being played on a radio station. R & B groups could not get their records played on "non" Black stations just like that. In order for a Black group to get its record played on a "non" Black station, its song needed to reach the number one slot on the Black charts. In addition to getting R & B groups' records played at Black stations like WDAS and WHAT, once a group performed at the Uptown Theater, DJs like Georgie Woods were able to get the big groups on American Bandstand, which was hosted by Dick Clark and located in Philadelphia. Once an R & B singer like James Brown performed on American Bandstand, he was able to cross over into mainstream, which typically meant instant success.

Hanging with many of the R & B singers and DJs at that time gave me a sense of importance. I was young, but felt blessed. I had access to living legends. I was living a life that a lot of kids would be envious of. I felt special.

God placed The Uptown in my life for a reason. Maybe because I was able to witness how The Uptown gave back to the community. Unc only charged 50 cents for the matinee shows, which were very popular due to the low cost. The 50-cent matinee was one way he give back to the community.

Also, at that time many people in the area would have no food and clothes. The Uptown would often give out food and clothes to those in need. They were all about giving back to the community, which is a value that was instilled in me.

Chapter 6:
Marijuana: The Drug of Choice

In 1970, The Comprehensive Drug Abuse Prevention and Control Act (US Controlled Substances Act) was passed by Congress, and placed marijuana into Schedule I, meaning it had no medical value and had the highest potential for abuse. However, marijuana continued to grow in popularity in the 70s, especially with the hippie culture. Sex and pot were not only popular with the hippies, they were also popular in the 'hood.

It was a sunny day on Cliveden Street in Mount Airy. I was hanging outside my apartment building sitting on the steps. "Hey Joey, how you doing?" I heard the little girl voice and turned around to look up at the apartment building next to mine. It was Donna, my cute classmate. Donna had long, pretty black hair, light caramel skin and a pretty face with a beauty mark. Her ethnic background was a mixture of White, Black and American Indian. I was attracted to her, but we never really hung out together, even though her apartment was next to mine.

So when Donna stuck her head out of her window to chat with me, I was excited. But then this boy approached Donna's apartment building and I saw Donna smile and blush. I had seen the boy before at my elementary school.

"Hey Joey, this is my boyfriend, Benny." I was devastated. Donna didn't open her window to chat with me, she was waiting for her boyfriend to arrive.

"What's up Joey," said Benny.

I responded, "Hi."

Benny was light-skinned with curly hair—the pretty boy type that girls liked. He and Donna were a great match physically, two very good-looking people.

I had no ill feelings toward Benny. Actually, I wished I were in his shoes. He had good looks and a pretty girlfriend. Somehow, Benny and I starting hanging out, which I enjoyed. We became very close. One day, we noticed that we both had bleeding sores on our arms from falling off our bikes earlier. "Hey Joey, hold your sore next to mine, so our blood can mix like they do on TV." That was our blood oath ceremony to take our friendship to a new level. We were blood brothers.

Benny's mom was a doctor and his pop was a lawyer, so they had money. Benny's parents owned a motel in Wildwood. I have fond memories of Benny and I hanging down Wildwood crabbing. We would catch the blue crabs off the pier and bring them back to the motel and cook them in the motel kitchen. Then we'd eat them for dinner. I had a blast hanging with Benny and his family.

Besides being good looking, Benny was also the type of kid who was good at everything. He was a pretty good guitar player. I was a pretty good drum player, and had been practicing since I received my first pair of drums for Christmas, when I was five years old. Benny and I used to

Power From Above

jam together and eventually we formed a neighborhood group with two other kids. We performed at our school and block parties. Benny and I were on top of the world! Okay, maybe not the world, but definitely the neighborhood.

Benny was a spoiled rich kid who, like myself, was exposed to weed at a young age and enjoyed getting high. Since Benny kept money, getting weed was never a problem. We hung out with the older kids and would attend several getting high parties. Holidays were big getting high days. I remember one New Year's night. It was cold as ice. We walked over to one of Benny's friend's houses and just got blasted. We were high as kites while listening to Parliament Funkadelic music. Getting high was becoming a way of life. As a kid, it all seemed fun. We didn't have a care in the world. Getting high and hanging with girls was our motto. And we felt indestructible.

Although life appeared to be good, getting high started to seriously conflict with my studies and my grades went down. I had always been a bright student with high grades. Weed and the classroom just weren't a good mix. Getting high made me feel like an adult, but I was really being immature by hurting myself in the classroom.

One day I was in school, high on weed as usual. Sitting in class, unable to even write one word, I could only scribble. At only nine years old, weed had made me lazy. I didn't study like I should have; goodbye A's.

Kids face many temptations in life. We give into temptations because they seem cool, or it appears that they will make us cool and fit in with others. Unfortunately, kids are sometimes too young to make good decisions, so they do things that they regret later. Sometimes, parents don't know what their kids are doing and don't realize their kids are out in the streets making bad decisions. Fortunately, there is one parent that sees all, God our Father.

Sometimes, divine intervention is required. In 1973, I was 10 years old, still getting high and hanging with the wrong crowd. It just so happens that my mom was saving money and finally raised enough to buy a house. By the end of 1973, we received a blessing from God and moved into our new house in a nice neighborhood in the Wadsworth section of Philadelphia. The neighborhood appeared to be very diverse, with low crime, but that didn't last long.

Chapter 7:
My New Hood

In November 1973, my mother, her boyfriend, my little brother and I, moved into our new row house in Wadsworth. Wadsworth seemed to be a nice area at the time. It was filled with row houses, which meant a lot of people per block. The racial makeup was 75% Black and 25% White. The White population decreased quickly within a few years.

My mother purchased our house from a White family that moved out to Montgomery County. White flight was common in Wadsworth during the late 1960s to early 1970s. At that time, many Whites had fear and anxiety about increasing minority populations. Many Whites sold their houses because they feared that their property values would decrease due to the influx of Blacks.

I personally witnessed many of the White businesses leaving the area. The barber shops and hair salons became Black-owned and all other businesses were brought by Koreans, including delis and beer stores. The public schools in the area were attended by 100% Black students.

I remember when I first walked down the hallways of Leeds Middle School. The walls were filled with pictures of graduating classes, all White. I was amazed how fast the school turned from all White to all Black in a matter of a few years. White flight.

On some levels, I can't blame some of the Whites who moved out of Wadsworth. Was their flight really due to the increase in Blacks, or was their flight due to the increase in violence?

It is a fact that as the increase of Blacks populated Wadsworth, so did the violence in the neighborhoods and schools. Many of the Blacks who came to Wadsworth were from many rough neighborhoods in the inner city. Although these families tried to escape the inner city to live in a better neighborhood, many of the kids were still tied to inner city gangs and did drugs.

Many of the issues I've faced in the past with violence and drugs followed me to Wadsworth. For me, it was a fresh start to get away from smoking weed and make some new friends. But my friend Benny visited me frequently and would always have a stash of weed. He and I would smoke in the back yard. Eventually, he met some of the friends I made in my new neighborhood and turned many of them on to weed. Before I knew it, I was getting high 24/7 again.

Darryl was one of my main friends in the new neighborhood. He was the type of guy everyone wanted to hang around. He was, like Benny, good at everything, especially basketball. When we played pickup basketball in the schoolyard, Darryl was always the first one picked for a team, and I was the last. I wasn't really good at basketball, because I never played it much before meeting Darryl. But I started to really enjoy playing basketball. However, I didn't appreciate being picked last to play. And I also didn't enjoy when kids busted on me for being a scrub. But I continued to play anyway. In the winter, we would even go out and shovel the snow and ice in the schoolyard so we could play basketball.

Although we primarily played basketball, we played other sports too, wall ball, wire ball, hand ball, half ball, and two hand touch football. We mostly played in our driveways or in the streets. Unfortunately, we didn't spend all of our time doing positive things like sports.

Darryl and I did a lot of bad things too—we got high, shoplifted, sold weed and were two of the top graffiti artists in the city. We use to steal bus passes at the bus depot and travel the city, getting high and writing on buses, train stations and walls—all at the ripe age of 11. If my mom had known I was walking through the subway tunnels with my friends, writing graffiti on the walls, she would have had a heart attack. For my friends and me, it was a thrill to know that people had to see our graffiti tag names as they rode the trains and buses. We all wanted to be like Cornbread, who is from Philadelphia and was regarded as the father of graffiti; his name used to be everywhere, including on an airplane.

I continued to do many bad things, without worrying about the consequences. I was even starting to bully kids in school. Many thought my crew and I were bad dudes. It was during this time that I lost sight of God. But God quickly showed me that there were consequences related to my actions.

One day, Darryl and I were walking around the neighborhood and found a $50 bill. We were excited.

"So what should we do with this money?" I asked Darryl. "Hmmm ... let me think. I know! We can buy some weed and sell it for a profit!" So we went to this guy we knew who was a weed dealer. We bought the weed and broke it down into $5 bags, known as nickel bags. We were ready to sell and try to double the money we found.

As we were walking down Washington Lane, in the West Oak Lane area, a Mr. Softy truck pulled to the side of the road, ringing its bell. Darryl and I approached the truck and asked to buy a few ice cream cones. On the truck were brothers in their twenties. They could tell we were high.

"Hey, you guys have some weed?" one asked.

"Yeah, we have some nickel bags for sale", Darryl replied. Like dummies, we let them feel several bags. They knew we were two high young kids who didn't know what we were doing. Once they had several of our bags in their hands, they laughed and drove off. There went all of our profit, which ended our short-lived weed business.

As if we didn't learn our lesson, we got into business with another friend, Antoine. We made $2.50 off of every $5 bag of weed we sold. Most times, we simply paid the $2.50 ourselves and got high. We would frequently get high over at Antoine's house, smoking up our profits.

One day, a bunch of us played hooky from school to get high over at Antoine's house. About eight of us went into his garage to wait for him to open the back door. We didn't realize a neighbor had seen us.

Power From Above

The next thing we knew, we heard sirens and a bunch of cars driving up to the driveway door. "Come out of there now!" we heard from the voices outside. "This is the police!" They started banging on the garage door, but we didn't budge. We were scared as hell. I looked behind me and one of the kids found a nice hiding place behind an old mattress. He was smart; I should have joined him.

Eventually, we caved in and open the garage door. You would have thought we were number one on the "Most Wanted List." I hadn't seen that many cop cars in my life. They quickly figured out that we were just a bunch of kids who knew the owner. Antoine stuck his head out of his kitchen window and finally admitted that he knew us. However, the cops took the opportunity to scare us straight. They placed us in handcuffs and took us to jail. We were locked in prison cells until our parents came and picked us up.

My mom was very disappointed. The last thing I ever wanted to do in life was disappoint her. We had gone through a lot together and she didn't need that type of drama.

God continued to show me the consequences of my actions. A bad-assed tough guy who got high all the time wasn't who I wanted to be. And it finally caught up to me one day in sixth grade. I was playing the tough guy role around one of my classmates. As I was walking down the stairwell, my classmate, Steve, was in front of me goofing around on the steps. I was trying to pass him.

"Yo Steve, move out my way, punk." This eighth grader was walking by and thought I was talking to him. It just so happens that this particular eighth grader was a football player, named Carl, who had other eighth grade football player friends.

He said to me, "Who you talking to?" Before I could say a word, he punched me in the eye. Blood started dripping from the cut above my eye. I was taken to the nurse and had to get butterfly tape. I looked like a boxer who was just in a fight, but I didn't get a chance to throw a punch.

Deep down inside, I knew I deserved that punch. It taught me that being a bully wasn't cool. It was like God punching me in the face himself and waking me up. He turned the tables and I was the one being bullied, but I never wanted to hurt anyone and God reminded me of that. The punch changed my life; it was another message from above. Don't be a bully, or you'll run into someone bigger and tougher than you.

After the incident with the eighth grader, the floodgates opened with cats trying to fight me left and right. I guess they saw a crack in my armor. One day, I was walking to school when, out of the blue, this older kid, a real tough looking guy, wanted to fight me.

He shouted, "Hey pussy, I'm going to punch you in the face!" I pulled out a set of my Bruce Lee inspired nunchucks I was carrying for protection.

One of my friends shouted, "Yeah Joey, fuck him up!" The kid still walked towards me, but cautiously. It gave me time to escape, because I really didn't want to hurt him. I had no beef with him. I just wanted to protect myself. No more punches to the face for me. That was life for me for the next few years, just trying to avoid fights.

This was a rough time for me. Although some people thought I was trying to be a tough guy, I was no fighter. It wasn't that I was scared; I just had no hate toward anyone. I was really a good guy at heart. I guess that's why the Lord never gave up on me. Somehow, I survived, but knew I had to change my life around and get away from the drugs and violence in the hood. I prayed.

As time went on, I got into fewer fights. One of the reasons is that God was answering my prayers. I was getting taller and more intimidating in size. I remember standing outside in line at a movie theater in the neighborhood; the gang members in our 'hood would go down the line, asking all the kids for money.

"Yo, give me some money," one of the gang members said to a kid next to me. The kid cooperated and gave him money. The gang member then looked me up and down, then passed me by and didn't say a word to me.

James Adams

I didn't let that go to my head. When I was getting into all of those fights, I made a promise to myself that I would no longer be a bully and only fight to defend myself. However, it didn't take long for me to get tested.

A few punks in the neighborhood were terrorizing little kids and also bothering some of the elders, my mom included. They would do stuff like throw eggs at our house at night, and they also would pick on my little brother, Jay, who was five years younger than I. The kids causing all of these problems were in their teens.

Days would go by and I stood by and never acted on their mischievous deeds. By no means was I scared of them, but I was trying to avoid fighting. I was trying to be a good person. I felt being good would eventually overcome evil. And these kids were evil.

One night, one of the bigger kids in the bunch was outside my back driveway, picking on my little brother Jay. That was the straw that broke the camel's back. I approached the kid named Al. At this point I felt I did everything to avoid confrontation, so when he said something to me, I punched him so hard, it knocked him to the ground.

"What you say, what you say," I screamed at him. "Get the fuck up," I shouted. He just laid there. That was the last of any problems my family and I had with that crew. Good did overcome evil. Now I was the one who had to punch someone in the face to teach them a lesson, just like the lesson I learned three years prior.

Chapter 8:
Basketball Saved My Life

The Youth Study Center (YSC) is the only secure youth detention facility in Philadelphia. The residents at the YSC are court-ordered juveniles between the ages of 13-18, who are alleged to have committed a felony type of offense and are deemed by the court to be a serious risk to the safety of the community. As I mentioned earlier, my friend George did some time at the YSC for shooting his father. In the late seventies, many of the cats from the neighborhood were either on drugs, committing crimes, at the YSC, or dead. Many Philadelphia teens were falling by the wayside.

During that time, I was able to graduate from Leeds Middle School in 1977 and was assigned to Germantown High School for ninth grade. I was falling into the same trap as others; I was on my way to falling by the wayside. Each morning before school, the cats around my way were either drinking or smoking weed. While traveling to school, we use to have the back of the bus lit up with smoke as we passed marijuana joints around. "Yo, pass the joint!" and sucking sounds were mostly heard. The bus was so crowded that people were getting high from just being in the back of the bus. To make things worse, I was in the advanced classes as a part of the magnet program for bright students.

James Adams

The only reason I was assigned to advanced classes was due to my high achievement test scores in middle school, but now I was in high school and needed better grades to stay in school and get my diploma. I had advanced biology first thing in the morning and would be so high I could not comprehend the teacher's lecture—I was surely on a path to failure and possibly flunking out of school.

One morning, the crew and I went to pick up our friend Ken before catching the bus for school. The doorbell rang. Ken answered the door.

"Yo Ken, you ready?" I said.

"Hold on a few, help me smoke this joint before we leave," he responded, turning around and going back down the hall. We chilled out in Ken's living room, smoking the joint. Ken then broke out some Southern Comfort. It was 7:30 a.m. and we were getting fucked up.

The next day, I had a test and decided to get to school early to hit the library. Later on that morning, I ran into Darryl in the hallway. His eyes were red and watery.

"What's up 'D,' you look high," I said.

"No man, I've been crying ... Ken shot himself this morning."

"What?? What happened?" I asked, shocked.

"We were getting high, then Ken pulled out his pop's shot gun ... started showing off and then—he pointed it to his head," Darryl paused for a moment as tears ran down his cheek. "He accidentally shot himself ... fucking blood splattered everywhere."

Power From Above

"Oh, shit!" I responded, in shock. I felt really bad that Ken had shot and killed himself, but a part of my shock was the realization that I could have been there, and what if he pointed that shotgun at me—my life would have ended just like Ken's life did. Getting high in the mornings before school was bad enough, but now someone was dead from being careless while he was high. Was God sending me another message? I thought so. I knew I had to get away from G-Town High School, which would allow me to get away from the boys in my 'hood.

It was at this time that I really discovered the power of prayer. I had developed a strong relationship with God and had prayed previously, but as I matured and confessed my sins and willingness to change my life, my prayers and relationship with God seemed to reach a new level. It appeared that God consistently answered my prayers.

I started to read the Bible more often and pray more often. I prayed every night, asking God to find me another school and get me away from all that was leading me down the wrong path in life.

During this time, Benny also attended G-Town. He had attended a different middle school, so we were back together again at the same school. Now we were older, and Benny was even more into the fast lane than before. He was still the pretty boy with money and good-looking girlfriends, but I no longer wanted to be in his shoes. We were starting to take different paths in life. One day, I saw him in the hallway at G-Town.

"Hey, what's up, Benny?" I asked him.

"I'm good, Joey. Hey, we're having a cocaine party this weekend, wanna' come?"

"Naw, I'm good. You into cocaine now? What's up with that?" I asked.

"Aw man, you need to try it, it's some good shit."

"I'll pass, but maybe we can hang out sometime like we used to," I said.

"Okay, cool; I'll catcha later."

We never did catch up later during that time, because Benny's favorite pastime was doing drugs, and that's what I was trying to get away from. But I still cared for and worried about him. He was my blood brother. We swore an oath to stay best friends forever.

One day after school, while waiting on the bus to go home, I noticed the Germantown YMCA. I remembered going swimming there with Benny a few years back. I decided to go over to the Y and inquire about a membership. I went home and gave my mom the details.

"Mom, can I get a membership to the Y? Here's the brochure." She took it and read it.

"Okay, we can afford a membership, and hopefully it will keep you out of trouble," my mom said, while seeming very excited about the idea. My mom was always very supportive and knew I was a smart kid who was trying hard to stay out of trouble.

"Thanks, Mom!"

Purchasing the Y membership helped save my life and got me away from drugs. The Y was also a catalyst to improving my basketball skills. God answered my prayers once again.

I went to the Y every day after school. I met new friends who were also into basketball and not into getting high. We pretty much lived at the Y. I was 14 and had never played organized basketball. At the Y, I played in my first league. Our coach was named Doc. When Doctor J hit town, several ballers adopted Doc as their nickname.

Doc formed the Y league. He would run us hard, but it was worth it. Doc introduced us to various basketball drills and they helped tremendously. He would shout, "Chest pass! Bounce pass! Overhead pass!"

Then if you messed up or goofed around, he would shout, "Give me 10 pushups!" Or even worse, "Give me one suicide!" Running suicides wore me out, but it got a guy in shape.

Doc eventually left the Y, and then entered Coach Ron. Ron was a young Caucasian guy who coached a well-known Philadelphia AAU team called the Sonic All Stars. He was hired by the Y as the athletic director, so we saw him every day. Eventually, Ron developed a 12-14-year-old team that included most of my friends and me. It was a match made in heaven.

Ron not only entered our team into nearby leagues, we also played in various tournaments at the Y, and on the road. My first tournament outside of Philadelphia was in Baltimore. Ron had entered us into a 15 and under tournament there. The competition was fierce. I never saw so many 15-year-olds who could dunk; those kids were jumping out of the building. I wouldn't have been surprised if there were a few ringers on their squad. They were way more advanced than us, but it was a great experience.

Although we were blown out of the tournament, we had fun. The hotel we stayed at was nice and that was the first time I ate at IHop. The pecan pancakes really hit the spot.

We went on to play in many tournaments and got better as time went on. Between playing ball at the Y every day and playing with the Sonics, my basketball skills increased dramatically as I grew taller. I was no longer a scrub. It got to the point that I could hang in games with the older ball players who played at the Y on adult night.

God brought basketball into my life and saved me. Basketball helped me to focus on the Bible and my schoolwork. I no longer had time for the potheads in my neighborhood. I could see the future. I now wanted to do well in school and play college basketball—that was my goal. And most important, I didn't want to disappoint my mother; I wanted her to be proud of me.

Power From Above

In order to play college basketball, I knew I first had to get good enough to make the high school team. But not at G-Town. There were too many distractions for me there.

One day, I happened to be driving with my older brother, Jack. He had to run an errand. As we were driving around, I noticed an area I'd never been in before. It was similar looking to Wadsworth; the houses looked the same, but with cleaner neighborhoods. There were also a lot of places to shop and eat. For some reason, I was attracted to the area. I asked my brother, "What's the name of this area?"

"It's called the Northeast," he responded.

"I wouldn't mind going to high school in this area." It was about a half hour from Wadsworth, so it was the perfect place to commute to high school. I felt it would be good for me to go to a school that didn't include anyone from my neighborhood so I could focus strictly on schoolwork and basketball.

When we got home, I immediately approached my mom with my idea. "Mom, Jack and I were in the Northeast part of Philly, and I would like to transfer to a school in Northeast." My mom was all for getting me away from the neighborhood. She caught me with a nickel bag of weed once, and confronted me about it, so she knew I smoked weed. But she also knew I was trying to get away from the bad influences in the neighborhood, so she was ready to make the high school transfer happen.

"Okay honey, I have a few connections. I know the school superintendent and will see if she can get your transfer processed." We researched several high schools in the Northeast area, including Washington and Lincoln, but Northeast High School seemed the most likely choice.

Unfortunately, there was a very long waiting list to get into Northeast if you didn't live in that area. At the time, the residents of the Northeast area were mostly White. Most of the Blacks who attended Northeast, were from other parts of the city, which made the waiting list long. When the odds seemed against me, I prayed about being accepted into NEHS and God answered. My mother's connections worked. I was accepted to Northeast for tenth grade.

Chapter 9:
Highschool Days

In the mid-1900s, the Northeast section of Philly had an influx of middle class families and was an almost completely White community. The Northeast had excellent schools, but minorities didn't have access to Northeast schools, because they didn't live in the area. In the 1970s, busing became a way to alter the racial imbalance there. Although busing created controversy among the Northeast residents, many of the Whites who were graduates of Northeast schools moved out of the area to the suburbs. This left room for minority families to attend Northeast schools, and some even moved into the area.

I entered Northeast High School in the fall of 1978. I was in tenth grade. Northeast was all I thought it would be. The kids seemed nice. I made new friends pretty fast, White and Black. I even saw a few kids I knew from middle school, and kids who had left Germantown like I did. Although Northeast was primarily made up of White kids, it was more culturally diverse than G-Town High, which was nice. This was the first time I went to a school that wasn't made up of at least 99% Black students. A more culturally diverse school at that time of my life was a blessing, because I knew it would help prepare me for a diverse college and more important, the real world.

At G-Town High, you had to worry about what to wear to school. It was like a fashion show. You were cool if you wore the latest fashions. During the time I attended, tweed pants with pleats and cuffed bottoms were the style. And you always had to keep a fresh haircut and expensive shoes.

Northeast High was completely different. It was a different culture. Unlike some of the kids at G-Town, many of the kids at NEHS didn't spend up all of their money on clothes. I was shocked to see people in jeans with holes in them, but that was a style. You would get laughed out of G-Town if you had holes in your pants, because people would think you were poor. At Northeast, if you wore jeans and a T-shirt, you were good, regardless of your economic status.

Before going to Northeast, I didn't know much about other ethnicities. When I arrived at Northeast, I quickly learned that Whites were made up of many ethnicities. It was during this time that I learned that some White ethnic groups made fun of other White ethnic groups. One day, I got off the bus and this white kid introduced himself to me.

"Hi, I'm David, what's your name?"

"My name is Joey."

After a lot of small talk, David said, "Hey, we should team up with you Blacks and kick the Jews out of Northeast." I didn't respond, mainly, because I didn't have a clue what the kid meant.

Later that day, I asked my Mom what David meant. She explained that some people were prejudiced against Jewish people because they didn't believe Jesus Christ was the Savior. After doing more research, I learned that Jewish people were the target of many White hate groups and had many of the same problems that Blacks had during the civil rights times and prior.

Northeast High helped open my eyes up to the importance of diversity and the understanding of various cultures and their identities. I discovered that Black and White didn't exist in solid biological foundation; in reality we all come from different nationalities and ethnic groups independent of color. The human race has various skin tones based on the amount of melanin in the skin. Ethnic groups which come from areas of the world with high sunlight intensity have darker skin color to protect them. I could never understand why people were prejudiced against each other based on skin color.

Except for the kid who made fun of Jewish people, based on my experience, everyone got along well at Northeast. I made some great friends. Since NEHS was around 90% White at the time, a lot of my friends were White and treated me very well. One time, I was talking with my classmate about his stamp collection and the next day, he gave me tons of stamps so I could start my own collection. Another time, I told this kid that I forgot my bus token and didn't have money to get home. He gave me his bus token and said he'd walk home. There were a lot of kind kids at NEHS who looked out for me—God placed me in the perfect school.

James Adams

I was accepted into Northeast in the tenth grade, a few months after school started. I was too late to try out for the basketball team, so I had to wait until 11th grade. Once my 11th grade year finally came, I was excited to get a chance to play high school basketball. After a few years playing at the Germantown Y and gaining some experience with the Philadelphia Sonics, I felt I was ready.

Basketball tryouts were fun. I quickly realized that the varsity team had most of its squad coming back with a few move ups from junior varsity. I had to secure a spot on JV. JV had a lot of returnees as well, so it was very competitive just to make the team.

Fortunately, I had a good tryout. I was confident I could make the team. Although some kids were a little more athletic and could jump high, my 6'5" frame helped me stay competitive on the boards. I also had a pretty nice jump shot.

After a few weeks of tryouts, Coach gathered us around him and talked about how hard all of us had worked, but he could only keep 12 players. He said, "I'll post the names of those who made it on the bulletin board tomorrow morning. For those of you who don't make it, thanks for coming out."

That night, I prayed to God to bless my family and friends, as I do each night. I also prayed for the power and strength to beat all odds and make the basketball team. "Please God, give me the ability to make the junior varsity basketball team, please be with me as I train and get better in basketball each day. In Jesus' name I pray!" As always, when I prayed, I felt a spiritual connection with God. I had faith that God would answer my prayer.

As Coach promised, the names of the players who made the team were posted outside the gym on the bulletin board the next day. I approached the board and looked for my name. YES! My name was there and I was overwhelmed with great joy. God had answered my prayers; I was now a high school basketball player.

My junior varsity year was fun and had its perks. We got out of class early for games, and traveled all over the city playing other high schools. We even had groupies. When we played some schools, we would get hit on by some of the girls. One day, we played Dobbins High School. There was a balcony looking down on the court.

"Hey number 45, you're cute!" one girl shouted at me from the balcony. "Want my phone number?" I just blushed.

My most memorable time playing JV was when I scored 15 points in one quarter against Lincoln High School. That was the most points I've ever scored in one eight minute quarter. I was unstoppable. Varsity, here I come.

James Adams

After my JV year, I continued to work on my game. Making the varsity team wasn't a definite yet; there were returning varsity members in addition to the guys who played JV. I had to make sure I was prepared for tryouts and stand out as much as possible. So during the summer, I worked out hard and prayed every night.

My 12th grade year finally came. My priorities were God, studying and making the varsity basketball team. So I continued to pray every night, read the Bible when I could, and hit the books. Basketball tryouts arrived, and I was ready.

Like the previous year, tryouts were pretty much running full court and making plays to stand out. This year, I had a JV resume, so I felt more comfortable. We finally reached the day to find out who made the team. Although I wasn't a definite, I felt I had done enough to make the team. But I knew there was a chance that some of the seniors who played JV last year, might not make the varsity team.

I approached the bulletin board that morning and saw my name—what a good feeling! I've experienced being cut before when trying out for the Sonny Hill league, so I knew what it felt like not to see your name on that list. Unfortunately, some of the guys I played with on the JV team did not make the varsity team and would not be able to play basketball their final year in high school. But I was one of the chosen ones. I was truly blessed. In both my 11th and 12th grade years, making the team was a long shot based on the numbers, but I survived the cuts both years. God answered my prayers.

Power From Above

Our team was made up of very good players. Although Northeast High was made up of only 10% Black students, our basketball team was 100% Black. When we entered the gyms of other high schools, teams and students were normally shocked, because they thought our team would be made up of White players. The Northeast area was widely known to be a predominately White area. Most of the good basketball players at the time were from other parts of the city—north Philly, west Philly and northwest Philly. Many of the players on our team were from these areas—they would play basketball 24/7. You didn't need much money to play basketball; you just showed up at the playground. In areas like the northeast, kids were exposed to many organized sports like baseball and didn't play as much basketball as their counterparts in the inner city. That's why Northeast's baseball team was made up of White players and our basketball team was the opposite. That's how things were.

Regardless of our ethnic makeup, our team was very good and had a great season. I had some good games and some games where I didn't play much. Although I didn't get the playing time I wanted, I was happy to be a part of the team. I prayed each night, hoping that I would make enough of an impact to get looked at by a small college.

I knew the key to my success was to pray, study and practice. I wasn't one of the stars of the team, but I knew I would play college basketball. I prayed to God; I prayed that I would get recruited to a small college where I could get a good college education and play college basketball. I knew that with God, it was possible.

James Adams

After a great season, our team was in the Philadelphia public league playoffs. Our record was 10-5. In the quarter finals, we had to play the number one team in the city, Franklin, whose record was 16-0.

The series of events that were triggered this day, strengthened my faith in God and confirmed what I already knew— God answered my prayers! No, I didn't make the game winning shot. We didn't even win the game. But something happened that would impact the rest of my life. The Coach started me. I hadn't started a game all season. I didn't get much playing time. But Coach decided to start me in the biggest game of the season.

I played the whole first quarter and can't say I scored a point, but played good defense. I blocked shots and rebounded. I played well enough to impress the Coach from Widener University. He was at the game to scout Ben, our star player, who ended up with 17 points and 12 rebounds in a 66 - 53 loss to Franklin. I didn't know the coach from Widener was interested in me until a few days after the game.

Coach called me to his office and told me the news. "We had a great season, Joey," he said.

I replied, "Yes we did, Coach, many people didn't think we would get that far."

Coach smiled. "The coach from Widener was at our playoff game and wants to talk with you. Here's his number," he said, handing me the man's business card.

I was so excited. It was getting close to the end of my senior year, and up to that point I didn't know where I was

Power From Above

going to attend college. I had prayed to God to bless me with a college offer, but no one was beating down my door prior to the playoff game against Franklin.

I called the coach from Widener and he set up a campus tour. He showed me around personally. I was being recruited to play basketball at Widener University, a division III powerhouse. When I returned from the Widener visit, I ran into another high school b-baller from MLK High School, named double D, and he gave me a significant invitation.

"Yo Joe, we're having AAU workouts for Martin's tonight at Gustine Lake. You should stop by."

"Okay, sure," I said.

I had never played AAU basketball up to that point, so I was game. Many of the best high school players across the nation played Amateur Athletic Union basketball, so it was nice exposure and great experience. I didn't think I would make the team, but I went to Gustine Lake anyway. Before entering the gym, I prayed that I would do well.

I entered the gym and saw nothing but all public/all city basketball players from various high schools across the city. But one thing that was surprising. When we started, it felt more like a practice than a tryout. I was under the impression that I was trying out, but it turns out the team was already formed. But it just so happens that one of G-Town's all-stars broke his ankle, so Martin's had a spot open. Just like that, I was on the team—playing AAU basketball for one of the top teams in Philly.

Martin's AAU team was coached by the great John Harnett. He was a good coach and a good person. He really looked out for his players. Once, after practice, I had a flat tire and I didn't have a spare. He drove my flat tire to Pep Boys and had it fixed.

Our first AAU tournament was at Mallory Rec Center. In my first game, I dominated the boards and led the team in rebounds. It was surreal. God had truly blessed me. I was playing against the best high school players in the city and holding my own—rebounding, blocking shots and scoring.

We won the tournament that weekend and I was a key factor. The next weekend, we had another AAU tournament in Fort Washington, PA. If we won, we would be the regional champs and move on to the national championship in Virginia. Unfortunately, the timing of the tournament was bad, because it was prom season and many of our players were hung over and had lack of sleep from attending proms.

To make matters worse, we had to play Mrs. Paul's, which was a team loaded with some all state and All American players. The game began; we tried to hang in the game, but we had no answers for Mrs. Paul's team. One of their players went up to dunk with his right hand, then switched it to his left hand, posterizing one of our players. They beat us. They deserved to move on with all that talent.

After the AAU season, my next goal was to play for the Sonny Hill league. I was cut from the team the previous year, but many of my friends played and I really wanted to make the team. Tryouts were in the northeast, not far from my high school. I did very well in tryouts and made it to the final 12 players, at least that's what I thought.

Power From Above

We played some scrimmages and I was the leading scorer in a few games. But that all changed when the All American players finished their AAU season. The big name high school players missed most of the Sonny Hill tryouts, but they really didn't have to try out—they were pretty much placed on the teams, which meant more cuts for the no name players.

Billy Thompson, an All American basketball player out of Camden High School, was placed on our team. Since I was the center at that time, I had to go up against him in practice. He took me to school. He was around 6'8" and had long arms, which made his wingspan around 7 feet long. He would back me up under the basket and just jump up like a polo stick and dunk on me. I couldn't stop him. He was the best player I played against up to that point.

Although he was making me look bad, I wasn't going out like that. He was sticking me about 10 feet from the basket. I blew by him and dunked the ball.

"My bad," he told his teammates.

I felt better, but knew my days on the team were numbered. I was cut to make room for the great Billy Thompson.

I was disappointed, because I was doing very well prior to going up against Billy Thompson. But it was a great experience. I would have eventually needed to leave the team, because that summer I was attending Widener University and was preparing for my first college basketball season by working out, reading the Bible and praying.

Chapter 10:
Playing With the Pros

Widener University is a small, private, co-ed university located in Chester, Pa. It's about 14 miles from Philadelphia. It was founded in 1821. In the late 1800's to mid-1900's, the University was a Pennsylvania Military College—also known as a PMC. By 1981, its name was changed to Widener University.

Although Widener is a small private university, it was a DIII powerhouse in basketball and football. Billy "White Shoes" Johnson was a football alumnus. The football team won the Stagg Bowl the year I entered in 1981. The basketball team was in the DIII final four in 1977. From that team, Dennis James was drafted by the Philadelphia 76ers.

I was really ecstatic that God answered my prayers and guided me to Widener University. It was the perfect school to get a great education and to fulfill my dream of playing college basketball. Although it seemed unbelievable that my prayers were answered, I always had faith.

In the summer of 1981, I started attending Widener University via the Act 101 program. PHEAA's (Pennsylvania Higher Education Assistance Agency) Act 101 program is a state-funded program which allocates funds to Pennsylvania schools that operate an Act 101 program at their institution. Schools use these funds to provide services to academically and financially disadvantaged students to assist them so they can successfully complete postsecondary study. My coach suggested that I attend the program in order to receive extra scholarship money.

I'm really glad I attended the Act 101 program. I think it really gave me a slight advantage over the new students starting in the fall. The program was a great orientation to the campus and I learned how to get around Chester and the surrounding area.

We lived in some of the new dorms on campus. My roommate was Ji, a very bright Korean student. I was very good at math and science, but Ji was on a different level. He used to help me to figure out chemistry problems. Ji also introduced me to ramen noodles and the hot pot. Ji kept a case of ramen noodles in our room and would cook them around 11:00 p.m. each night. They used to smell so good, and I was usually hungry around that time of night, because we would eat dinner early, around 5:00 p.m.

"Hey Ji, you mind if I have some of those noodles?" I'd ask.

"Sure," he'd say as he dropped an egg in the hot pot with the noodles. Ji was like a ramen noodle chef—he hooked them up.

Some of the other Act 101 students lived in Chester, which had a reputation for its high crime areas, poverty and violence. All of the people I've met from Chester were fine with me. There was this one girl named Tina. She lived in Chester and had an older boyfriend who was in his late 40's, about 30 years older than her. He would come up to visit her often. He was a weird guy. He would walk around barefoot in his martial arts uniform. We heard that he'd fought in the Korean War. He appeared to be the jealous and overprotective type, so I'm sure he didn't like Tina hanging out with the guys in our program that were Tina's age.

Tina and I would often sit in the dorm lobby to study together. We became friends, but nothing more. Although I was single at the time, her boyfriend visited often and as I mentioned previously, he seemed a little weird . . . everyone felt something was off with him. One day, Tina asked me to walk her to the cafeteria to eat lunch. We walked out of the dorm.

"Oh, I forgot my ID. You go ahead, I'll catch up," she said.

So I continued to the café and Tina ran back into the dorm to get her student ID.

I entered the café, got my food and sat down to eat. Tina never caught up with me.

As I was sitting in the cafeteria eating lunch. Several of the Act 101 students started running into the cafeteria, screaming, "Tina was shot!" By the time we went outside, police were everywhere. We saw them handcuffing Tina's boyfriend, while Tina lay dead in the Old Main parking lot. Witnesses saw Tina's boyfriend shoot her. After he shot her, he sat on the ground with his legs crossed until the police came to arrest him. We later found out that he killed her because she wanted to break up with him. What a tragedy.

James Adams

My mom called me shortly after the news hit the Philly networks. "Hello," I answered.

"Joey, are you okay?" she asked.

"Yes, I'm fine. Tina was killed by her boyfriend," I told her.

"That's so sad. When I heard the news, the only thing I heard was, "Teenager shot at Widener University," and then I freaked out. I'm glad you're okay." My mom was so happy to hear that I was okay, but I often wonder what would have happened if I was walking Tina to the dining hall that day when she ran into her jealous boyfriend. If Tina hadn't forgotten her ID, I would have been with her and my life could have been over, just like Tina's. I believe I literally dodged a bullet that day. I feel divine intervention was the reason.

In spite of Tina's tragic death, I enjoyed myself. Living at Widener opened my eyes to a whole new world and I was meeting people from all walks of life, including professional athletes. The Philadelphia Eagles held a summer camp at Widener. At the time, Ron Jaworski was the Eagles' quarterback. One day, I was walking to my dorm room and saw Ron approaching.

"Hello," I said, delighted.

He smiled and said, "Hello," as we walked past each other. I didn't want to act like a crazed fan, so I just played it cool. It's a little surreal when you meet people you're used to seeing on TV all the time. Meeting "Jaws" was only the beginning. A few days later, I looked outside my dorm room, which overlooked a track, and saw Sixers 6'11" center, Caldwell Jones, jogging around. The Sixers was my favorite basketball team, so I was in awe seeing Caldwell in person.

In September, 1981 the fall semester began at Widener University. I moved into my dorm room and started my college life. Life was good. I studied, played basketball and partied. My friends and I would go on road trips to other local colleges in the middle of the week. College was awesome.

Basketball practice was set to start October 15th. I was really excited to start my first college basketball season. But something happened that overshadowed my excitement to get my college basketball career started.

Although seeing Caldwell Jones in person was great, one of my favorite Sixers players was Darryl Dawkins. I really loved the way he would dominate in the paint and periodically broke the fiberglass backboards. They used to have a show on TV that allowed average people to fulfill their dreams and play against a professional athlete. I always dreamed I would play against Double D—Chocolate Thunder.

God continued to answer my prayers. I was recruited to the school where the Sixers practiced. Fitz Dixon was a long-time owner of the Sixers and chairman of the board at Widener University. Although Fitz had just sold the Sixers to Harold Katz that summer, the Sixers were used to practicing at Widener. That's why Caldwell Jones used Widener's track for jogging. Although they were about to move to another practice location the following year, many of the Sixers came up to Widener University to get in shape before their training camp.

Before I knew it, I was playing pickup basketball games with Darryl Dawkins, Earl Cureton, Clint Richardson, and several of the Sixers' draft picks. About four years prior to this time, I was playing pickup games with my friend "Darryl" from the neighborhood, I was being called a scrub, and was the last person picked to play basketball in the school yard. Nobody wanted me on their team, but now I was playing pickup games with another Darryl—Darryl Dawkins and other NBA players. That was a major upgrade between Darryls and other players. The power of prayer and hard work was in full effect.

During one game, I played on Darryl Dawkins's team. He was sticking Earl Cureton. I was sticking Clint Richardson. Clint shot a layup. I pinned it against the backboard.

Darryl Dawkins looked at me and said, "Good defense."

I looked back and said, "Thanks." That made my year! To me, at that time Darryl Dawkins was bigger than life—not only due to his 6'11" 250 lb. frame, but he was the first player I saw shatter a backboard in the NBA.

Power From Above

In 1979, I was watching the Sixers play the Kansas City Kings. During one play, Maurice Cheeks passed Darryl the ball down low and Darryl threw down such a massive dunk that the backboard shattered. The glass started falling on the Kings' Bill Robinzine, which sent him ducking and running for cover. Three weeks later, Darryl broke another backboard. The NBA had to start using breakaway rims; Darryl changed the game and I was now playing on his team.

Darryl and some of the other Sixers were pretty cool. They were down to earth. I had been watching Darryl play for the Sixers since I was 14 years old, when he and the Sixers were playing Portland in the 1977 NBA championship, he seemed so much older, but he was only six years older than I was. So at this time, I was 18 years old and Darryl was only 24. When I hung out with him, he talked to me like one of the homies from the 'hood.

One day, Darryl said, "Hey man, come out to the van for a few."

I said, "Sure." Darryl would have coolers filled with brew in the back of his van. It was great to chill out after some pickup games and have a cold one. Wow, what a life——playing pickup games with one of your favorite NBA players, then chilling out with him over a cold beer afterwards—this was like heaven on earth for a teenager—at least it was for me.

Darryl was a DJ on the side and used to invite me, and some of the other Widener players, to his parties in Jersey. God not only guided me to a school where I could get a good education and play basketball, he guided me to a school where I could get to know one of my favorite Sixers. God made it possible—he answers all prayers.

I called Benny to tell him about my pickup games. Benny would have loved to be there with me.

"Hey Benny, guess what, man?"

"What?"

"I've been playing pickup games with some of the Sixers," I told him.

"Oh yeah?" Benny was excited for me.

"Yup! I've been playing with Darryl Dawkins, Earl Cureton, Clint Richardson, and a bunch of the Sixers' draft picks. Doc hasn't shown up, but I've also seen Caldwell Jones running around the track and I just saw Billy Cunningham talking to Bobby Jones down near the locker rooms."

"Wow, that's great, Joey, I wish I was up there with you," he told me, shaking his head in admiration.

"Yeah, me too ... how are things going with you?"

Benny replied, "I'm good. I've been hustling, making money boxing, partying, you know me, gots to party!"

When Benny said he was partying, I knew he was still hitting the drugs.

"Hey Benny, if you want to be a great boxer, you got to train hard and give up that partying, and make sure you pray, my brother. It worked for me; I'm here playing with the pros and about to start my college basketball career, and I believe it all happened because of prayer."

Benny responded, "Hey look Joey, I gotta' go. I'll catch you later."

"Okay, later," I replied. I hoped my message to Benny didn't go into one ear and out the other.

Chapter 11:
BBall: College Style

Under NCAA (National Collegiate Athletic Association) rules, October 15th signals the official start of practice for college basketball teams. On Thursday, October 15, 1981, I attended my first college basketball practice.

Since we had been playing pickup games for the past month, I was already impressed with the nice locker rooms, showers, training room and other parts of the facility. It was a major upgrade from high school. We had a trainer on hand if we wanted to get taped. All of our practice clothes were ready for us in our lockers. I was taped, dressed and ready to go.

Before practice, we had a short meeting in the remedial room. Coach handed us the itinerary that included basketball quotes to live by, training/conditioning demands and suggestions, and practice tips. Coach stressed the importance of practice. He pointed out to us, "Games are won on the practice floor."

Practice started and went well. I quickly learned that Coach was a drill sergeant. A perfectionist. If you screwed up, you heard about it. I remember running a play, and making a mistake. Coach let me have it.

"Joey! What the fuck are you doing! If you can't run the fucking play right, you're running suicides all fucking day!" I had to learn not to take his outbursts personally. He was known for making players walk out of the gym after his famous tongue-lashings.

For the first couple of weeks, we hardly picked up a basketball. We did a lot of drills and running. The suicide runs weren't my favorite. A suicide run is when you have to start at the baseline, then run to the foul line, back to the baseline, then to half court line, back to baseline, then to far foul line, back to baseline, then to opposite base line and back to starting baseline. And don't come in last, because if you do, you have to do it again. I wasn't the fastest guy on the team, so I would hear, "Joey! Hustle, hustle ... don't come in last!"

I actually loved the preseason practices. They got me in shape and helped improve my basketball skills. In high school, our practices were primarily scrimmaging and going over a few drills. I loved my high school coach, but Coach C. knew how to run a practice and get the best out of you. I'm sure he learned a lot from observing the Sixers practice for several years.

The season started and we were ready to go. In the late 70s and early 80s, Widener University was a Division III basketball powerhouse. Widener basketball teams not only played DIII teams, but DI and DII teams as well. There were some players on our team who could have started for several DI teams. Coach was a good recruiter and knew how to pick good, talented players for his program.

Power From Above

My first year, the varsity team was packed, so I had to play JV, but I didn't mind. I got a chance to play against several community and junior colleges. JV basketball was fun. No expectations—just play ball and gain some experience to prepare for the varsity team. I used JV games and practice to my advantage. I wanted to impress Coach to show him I belonged on the varsity team. I averaged around 20 points and 10 rebounds a game.

The following year, I got my chance to play varsity. We started out of the gate strong. We beat the first three teams by an average of 23 points. We were 3 and 0. Then we played Penn State, an Atlantic 10 DI school. Penn State had a very good team. Before we played them, they beat Maryland 97-79 and Indiana (PA) 84-46. Their top two big men were 6'9" and 6'11" tall. Both were averaging in double figures. They were 2-0, we were 3-0 ... someone had to lose.

We arrived at Penn State's gymnasium. We walked in and I had to just pause and take it all in. It was the biggest basketball stadium that I'd played in up to that point. I looked up and saw the flags from all the D1 teams in the A10 conference. This was big-time.

We walked into the huge locker rooms. We had sliced oranges, sodas and snacks set aside for us to use at half-time and after the game. D1 players were treated so much better than D3 players. It wasn't a surprise, because D1 basketball programs bring in so much revenue. After soaking it all in, we got dressed for the game and were ready to go.

Penn State's coach was interviewed before the game and said, "Widener has four division I players in their starting lineup. I've known their coach for years and I know how bad he wants this game. They have an overall solid team and will be a good test for us."

And test them we did. We played them like we belonged in the Atlantic 10 conference. By half-time, we were only down by a few points and we heard their coach blasting them in a nearby locker room. He was saying things like, "You're supposed to be one of the top 25 DI teams this year and you're letting a DIII team hang in the game, and their star player has 18 points at half-time."

For that night, God let me know how it felt to play ball at the highest level of college basketball. I enjoyed being able to embrace the moment of our team playing on the D1 level. I was no longer a little kid playing basketball in the 'hood. I was no longer a high school basketball player. This was a much higher level of basketball. God answers prayers. As God answered prayer after prayer, I not only had deep and strong faith in him, I had trust in God and knew I was being led in the right direction.

Penn State beat us that night by 18 points, but it didn't matter. We knew our team could hang with the best. Our next big test was another A10 team, University of Rhode

Power From Above

Island. The URI basketball team included three former Philadelphia Public League standouts, Horace Owens, Kevin Compton and Terry Pittman. Terry and I were friends. We played on John Hardnett's AAU basketball team together.

We played another great game against a DI team. URI only beat us by 9 points. That was our third loss of the season—two losses to DI teams. At that point, the experience gained by playing a couple of DI teams helped us to dominate our DIII division. At the end of the season, we were 20 and 7, winning our conference championship.

After our conference championship, we played in the NCAA Regional Championship. We beat our first game against Grove City. We lost to the University of Scranton in the championship game. Scranton had a very good team that year. Had we got by Scranton, I think we would have won the NCAA DIII championship. As a consolation, we received plaques and certificates for being the 1983 NCAA DIII Regional second place team.

Overall, it was a great season for our Widener University basketball team. My first year on the varsity team was successful. I had a great experience. I had come a long way from being a last pick for a pick-up game of basketball in the neighborhood. With hard work and prayer, I achieved my goal— playing college basketball and getting a good college education. Once again, God answered my prayers.

Chapter 12:
Meeting My Soulmate

Most co-ed universities in the United States have a higher percentage of females attending than males. If you're a male, there's a good chance you will find a girlfriend in college. At the least, you will experience a hookup. Universities are the perfect environment to meet someone in class, in the cafeteria, at campus events, at parties—anywhere on campus.

Prior to college, I had never had a girlfriend. Not that I couldn't get a girl. There were girls who had a crush on me and there were girls I had a crush on, but I was very picky and never was able to find that special girl I could call my girlfriend. During my first couple of years at Widener, the floodgates had opened. I was not only meeting girls at Widener, but my friends and I would take road trips to nearby universities and I would meet girls there, too. And that wasn't all. Girls at Widener would have their girlfriends visit them at Widener and I would meet them too. It was crazy!

I was young, on the basketball team, getting a good education and meeting girls left and right; life was good. Although I was meeting several girls, at the start of my second year at Widener, I was starting to feel like settling down with that special girl. I wanted a meaningful relationship. I would call my friend Benny, the ladies' man.

"Hey, what's up Benny?"

"What's up Joey!" Benny always sounded excited to hear from me, even if we had spoken recently. That's the type of guy he was; he would walk in a room and light it up. He knew how to make a person feel good just by talking with them.

"I'm still trying to find that right girl, Benny," I said.

"Joey, you're down there with those fine college honeys and you can't find a girl?"

"I can find a girl, but I want to find the right girl for me ... I'm not like you. I can't just mess around with girls to get laid; you run through girls like water."

"You crazy Joey, we're young. This isn't the time to get strapped down with one girl." Benny just cared about getting high, getting paid and getting laid. I loved the dude, but he was the wrong person for advice on settling down with one girl.

In fall of 1982, a new crop of girls entered Widener. It was time to scout out the new girls and see if there was a special girl for me. I met a girl named Holly at the Black Student Union party. She was very dark-skinned and wore very colorful clothes.

"Hello, you want to dance?" I asked her.

"Yes," she said.

I asked her, "What's your name?"

"Holly," she smiled at me.

Power From Above

"Nice to meet you, Holly." We danced, and then went back to her room after the party to make out.

Holly and I dated for most of my sophomore year, but deep down inside, I knew she wasn't the right person for me. Our relationship was primarily physical. Beyond that, we didn't have much in common and I became bored hanging with her. I would do things to push her away, like not speaking to her for a few days. I would come up with things to argue about—I would make her cry and she would then write me a nice letter, saying how much she cared about me. It would suck me right back in line and we would make up and have some good times having sex.

Eventually, I guess she got the message; I no longer wanted to date her. I stopped speaking to her and she moved on to one of the other basketball players on the team. One day at practice, Coach huddled us up after practice. He went over our plans for the winter break. He said, "So who is Holly going home with over the break, Joey or Darrell?" Everyone laughed, because everyone knew I had recently dated Holly, and now Darrell was fucking her. Coach knew about Holly and Darrell, because they were both in the math class he taught.

Many of my friends teased me and said I turned Holly out, which meant that I used her for sex and turned her into a ho. She was not only fucking Darrell, but she would get drunk and sleep with a lot of guys on campus. When Holly and I met, she had a boyfriend. She had his picture hanging up in her room, but when we started dating, the pictures eventually came down. Maybe that was the feeling I had deep down inside; if she cheated on him, she would eventually cheat on me. Luckily, I bailed out of the relationship before that happened. I prayed for the right girl to enter my life. God let me know that Holly wasn't the one.

The summer of '83 hit and I was still without a girlfriend. I worked in a Social Security office in Philadelphia. Between working and training for the upcoming basketball season, I stayed busy. But I really wanted to find the right girl—my soul mate. I prayed to God about it every night.

Once again, in the fall of 1983, the new crop of girls entered Widener and once again, I was optimistic to meet a nice girl. On the first day of classes, another teammate and I went to lunch in the cafeteria. And there she was, the girl of my dreams. She was a pretty, light brown-skinned girl with tight jeans. Her ass looked good in those jeans. I quickly went over and introduced myself and Cube.

"Hello, what's your name?" I asked.

"Elle, what's yours?"

"I'm Joey and this is my teammate, Cube."

"What sport do you play?"

"Basketball, do you like basketball?"

"Yes," Elle responded.

"Good, hopefully you can come out to check out some of our games."

"Sure."

Cube and I sat down to eat, but I kept thinking about Elle. I kept glancing over to check her out as she ate with her roommate. I was immediately attracted to her because she carried herself like a lady and I could tell she was a classy girl. She was the kind of girl you can take home to mom.

Later that evening, I saw Elle again. I was sitting outside my apartment with Cube and my two roommates, LJ and Rye. LJ was the star of our basketball team and Widener's all-time scorer at the time. We later found out that we are cousins by marriage. In other words, we have the same first cousins. LJ and I were close from day one, but finding out we were cousins created a stronger bond between us. Rye wasn't on the basket- ball team, but was a pretty cool dude. LJ and Rye were roommates together my freshman year. I used to practically live in their dorm room, which led to all three of us getting an apartment together.

My apartment was down the street from Howard Johnson's, aka, Ho Jo's, which was a restaurant that sold ice cream. Elle was walking back from Ho Jo's and had to walk right by my apartment.

"Hello, ladies," I said.

"Hi Joey." Elle and her friend chatted with us for a while and went back to their room.

Widener was a small campus, so I knew I'd see Elle pretty often. I found out that she was single. I started to visit her room to hang out with her. Her parents kept her stocked with snacks and she had a popcorn maker. I always got hungry around 11:00 p.m., so it was nice to hang out with Elle and eat some popcorn; chips and pretzels were our favorites.

James Adams

We started to develop a nice friendship. It took me a while to get close, because she wasn't the type of girl who was flirty. At times, she seemed shy and a little standoffish. I didn't push it; I let her have her space. I was more interested in her personality.

The whole fall semester was a getting to know each other period. It was nice, because we got a chance to develop a friendship, which gave our relationship a solid foundation. A solid foundation is very important. It's like the story about "The Three Little Pigs." One pig built a house of straw, one pig built a house of wood, but the smartest pig built a house of brick so that the wolf couldn't blow his house down. With relationships, if you don't build it with a strong foundation, it will eventually be destroyed. I had already built a strong relationship with my family and God, so I knew how important it was to have one with my future soul mate.

When we returned to Widener in spring 1984, our relationship grew to another level. "So Elle, we've been friends

Power From Above

now for about four months. Do you want to be my girlfriend?" That was the first time I asked a girl that question.

"Yes," she replied timidly, but with a smile. The funny thing is, we hadn't had sex yet. We'd made out, but no sex. I respected that, but when the time came, I knew I would be her first and only.

Although I knew God had finally brought the right girl into my life, I would still do dumb things to try to push her away. I had finally realized that I wasn't used to being committed to someone. I was used to being single—doing my own thing. But Elle wouldn't let my antics push her away. She really cared for me and didn't let me run away from our relationship. God answered my prayers—Elle was meant to be my soul mate. Although I prayed for the perfect girlfriend, I never thought it would happen, but God knew. God led me to basketball, which then led to Widener and then to Elle.

Chapter 13:
Joining the Frat

A fraternity is a brotherhood, a group of men associated or formally organized for a common purpose. In the early 1900's, several Black men came together at a few universities, and formed Greek letter fraternities. Their purpose was to cater to and provide support for Black college students who had no actual support system of their own at their institution.

In the early 1900s, Blacks at predominantly White institutions had to deal with racism and didn't have the resources like their White counterparts. By creating a fraternity, Blacks could now pull together their resources and find ways to survive on campus instead of falling by the wayside due to lack of resources, racism and other challenges they faced.

By the late 1900s, the Black fraternity memberships grew to thousands of members and were made up of doctors, lawyers, teachers, politicians, sports athletes and more. Martin Luther King, Ralph Abernathy, Leon Sullivan and Wilt Chamberlain were Black Greeks, just to name a few.

My first contact with Black fraternities was in the late seventies, when I was in high school. Philadelphia was host for the annual Greek picnic, which was held each summer in July. The Greek picnic was not only popular with Greeks, but was also popular with curious high school students like myself. I used to go to the picnic with my friend and high school basketball teammate, Mack.

Mack and I had a blast at the picnic. We weren't Greek, but there were so many fine babes there, it didn't matter. But most of all, we got a chance to see the brotherhood and good times shared amongst the fraternities. Mack and I quickly knew which fraternity we wanted to be a part of; we wanted to be Kappas. They were cool and the women loved them.

"Yo, Mack, I want to be a Kappa."

"Me too, those brothers are smooth."

"I know ... and they do a lot for the community."

With each visit to the annual Greek picnic, our desire to become a Kappa became stronger. We couldn't wait to start college and join the frat. After high school, Mack enrolled at the University of Pittsburgh. Fortunately for Mack, Pitt had a Kappa chapter there. Widener did not.

In the fall 1983, around the same time I met Elle, Mack called and told me the good news. "Yo Joey, I'm about to be pledged to Kappa."

"That's great Mack, good luck man, you can do it. Stay strong."

"Thanks, Joe, wish you were going on line with me," Mack answered

"Thanks Mack, I do too. I'm hoping we can get a chapter started here at Widener next year. In the meantime, at least one of us is getting a shot to pledge. I'll talk to you when it's over."

"Okay, Joe."

Later that fall, Mack was a Kappa.

It was my fourth and final year. I felt blessed. I was playing basketball, I had a great girlfriend and I was close to getting my B.S. degree. I was missing one thing—I wanted to be a Kappa like my boy, Mack. Ironically, a Kappa from Pitt transferred to Widener my senior year. He was one of the Kappas who pledged Mack. He tried to help me and a few other students pledge at a nearby university, but that fell through and my chance to pledge Kappa as an undergrad faded.

Since I couldn't pledge Kappa my senior year, I decided to focus on my academics, so I could graduate on time. Due to too many road trips and partying, my grades weren't the best. Unfortunately, in order for me to buckle down and graduate on time, I made the decision to quit the basketball team. I loved playing basketball and I loved my teammates, but I knew I had to make that sacrifice.

It just so happens that the team went to the D3 final four that year. I still practiced with the team from time to time, so I still felt a part of the team and was rooting for them to win a NCAA D3 championship, but I enjoyed the additional time I freed up by not playing. I was able to establish a stronger relationship with Elle, plus work on my grades. Another factor was that if I didn't graduate on time, I could come back another year to play basketball and not be in the shadows of our 6'10" starting center.

James Adams

The extra time focusing on my studies worked. I wasn't able to graduate in May, because I needed to complete two more courses. But things came full circle when I was able to stay on campus during the summer as an ACT 101 counselor and complete my final two courses. In August 1985, I graduated from Widener University with a B.S. Degree in Science Administration.

To celebrate my graduation, Benny and a few of my friends took me out for some drinks and food. Benny broke out the weed and cocaine, but I wanted no part of the drugs. I never experienced cocaine and never wanted to experience it either. For me, I didn't need to get high in order to celebrate or have a good time. I was already high on the many blessings I'd received in life. The weed smoking days were behind me. Unfortunately, Benny depended on drugs for his high. Benny represented the road not taken by me. I'm not saying I didn't flirt with going down that road, but as Benny and I got older, we were on two distinct roads.

As we were riding in the car in downtown Philly, we saw a bunch of hot women walking the streets. As many horny young guys do, some of my friends felt the need to holler out the window while we were driving, "Hey baby, what's your name?" Rex shouted. "Can I get some fries with that shake?" He was throwing out all of the corny one liners that were so cliché.

Rex caught the eye of this hot looking lady on a corner. She was dressed in a short mini skirt with her boobs popping out of her blouse. Rex pulled the car closer to the curb to talk to the lady.

"Hey baby, want to party?"

She responded, "Sure."

I thought the guys were just joking around with her, but Benny made a mistake and said, "Hey pretty lady, how much to party with all four of us?"

She responded, "How about $100?"

Then Benny fucked up and agreed and the next thing I saw was the lady reach into the car and take the car keys. She was an undercover cop.

All of a sudden, we're riding in a cop wagon and I'm spending the night in jail because of Rex and Benny. I explained to the police that I just graduated from college and we were out just having a little fun. The arresting policeman was pretty cool; when he wrote up the paperwork, he didn't use my real name.

As I was sitting in the jail cell, the walls felt like they were caving in on me—I was feeling claustrophobic and I was pissed that I was in this predicament after working so hard to stay on the right path in life. I knew I couldn't let this happen again.

In the morning, we just had to pay a fine and they let us go. Sure, spending the night in jail was crappy, but the thing that bothered me the most about that night was Benny's drug habit. He was out of control and I knew he was on the path to self-destruction. I cared for my friend Benny and tried to talk some sense into him, but it would go into one ear and out of the other. It came down to him wanting to help himself. Unfortunately, I had to start separating myself from him, because if the police would have found drugs in the car, we could've received more than a fine for soliciting prostitutes.

The next day after being released from jail, I decided to go to a nearby recreation center and play some basketball to blow off some stress from being arrested over some dumb shit. I ran into Raj, the recreation director. He was going in his office as I was walking by.

"Hi Joey, how's it going?"

"Fine, just came to play a little ball." Raj was now in his office and I was standing at the doorway. I noticed a Kappa Journal on his desk.

"I didn't know you are a Kappa!" I said, surprised and excited.

"Yeah man, what you know about Kappa?" Raj said jokingly.

"I wanted to pledge while I was at Widener, but that fell through, and we don't have a Kappa chapter on campus."

"Why don't you pledge grad?" Raj asked.

"I checked with the city alumni chapter and they're not having a line this year."

"You don't have to wait for the city chapter, there's a suburban chapter starting soon. Here, give this brother a call." Raj gave me the number to a brother who pledged with him during his undergraduate years. I called as soon as I got home.

The Kappa explained that the suburban chapter was starting a line that upcoming January. It would be the first line of the newly formed suburban alumni chapter. God had answered my prayers! If I could make it through the initiation process, I would be a Kappa man!

That spring of 1986, I went through the initiation process for several weeks and on June 21, 1986, I became a Kappa. In a five year span, I played high school basketball, graduated high school, played with NBA players, played college basketball, met the love of my life, received a B.S. degree, and became a Kappa man. All by the age of 23 years old. I was so blessed. I knew God was watching over me. I could have easily died when I was hit by that car when I was four years old, but that wasn't in God's plans.

Unfortunately, Benny continued to go down a path of destruction. Drugs and the fast life were catching up to him. He and I visited church together when we were younger. I prayed that he could develop a strong relationship with God, because if he didn't change his life, he would die an early death.

Chapter 14:
Crack

In the late 1970's, there was a huge amount of cocaine imported into the United States. As a result, the price started to go down. Drug dealers used the cocaine powder to make small rocks called crack. Crack was a cheap substitute for cocaine and it gave people a quick and potent high—it was very addictive.

The crack epidemic hit many U.S. urban cities, including Philadelphia, between 1984 and 1990. The drug turned its users into "crackheads," who looked like zombies jonesing for a fix. But the drug was very lucrative for drug dealers. The urban areas were filled with drug dealers who had Mercedes autos and BMWs with the spoilers. But the drug dealers didn't have it that easy. With drugs, money and power came violence. Crack- heads were ruining their lives while on crack and the drug dealers were living a fast life and were either placed in jail or dead at a young age.

Crack affected my life because I saw many of my friends ruin their lives by taking that poison, including Benny. After I graduated from Widener University, while crack was in the 'hood pretty heavy, Benny met this girl named Tanya in north Philly. The girl was nice looking, but she was starting to use crack. At that time, Benny was trying to get his life together and chill out on using drugs. His boxing career was going okay and he was making some good money. After hooking up with Tanya, things started to go downhill again. Tanya, like Eve, was holding forbidden fruit to tempt Benny.

The first time Benny visited Tanya, he was excited and hoping to get some booty. Benny pulled up to Tanya's door and knocked. Tanya answered the door, "Hi baby, come in." They hugged. As Benny walked in, Tanya's mom, her mom's boyfriend, sister and brother were in the living room getting high on crack.

"How ya'll doing?" Benny greeted them.

"We're good, come in and make yourself comfortable. Here pull up a chair," Tanya's mom said.

Tanya joined in. "Here baby, try some."

"Naw, I'm cool."

"Come on, this shit is all that."

Benny had used cocaine before, but never crack. It didn't take him long to give in—and soon he was another victim of the crack epidemic. Tanya and Benny got high and went upstairs and had hot sex while they were both high as kites.

Over the next several months, Benny practically lived over at Tanya's house, which pretty much turned into a crack house. Getting high and having sex—this was the life for Benny. The mom and the rest of the family loved Benny because he was using his boxing money to buy crack. That made him a popular dude. But eventually, Benny's boxing career started to fizzle due to not training and not showing up for actual fights because he was too high in Tanya's crack house. Benny was now a crackhead, and like other crackheads, he would do anything for that next high.

One day, I received a call from Rex. "Hey Joe, guess what happened?"

"What?"

"Benny just got arrested for breaking into his cousin's house. A neighbor saw him climbing in a window and called 911. The cops caught him red-handed, coming out of the house with his cousin's stereo in his hands."

"Wow, that's a damn shame ... he stole from his own cousin...how low can you get?" I shook my head. "I really feel sorry for him."

"Yeah, me too," Rex replied.

Benny was just one of many of my friends who fell prey to crack. Many old-heads I looked up to were now walking around with a dirty bucket and rag, trying to make a few dollars washing cars so they could get high. I prayed for them, but I was blessed that God made me strong enough to stay away from drugs. Although I used to smoke weed, I never tried cocaine or crack. I dodged that bullet. God answers prayers and "with God, all things are possible."

Chapter 15:
With God, All Things Are Possible

I often look at the world and marvel at the mechanics that keep us alive each day. The sun is the perfect distance from Earth to keep us warm and provide us with light—and is so important for our plant life. Gravity is not seen, but plays a major role in our everyday life. It literally keeps us grounded. Oxygen is also not seen, but we breathe it in 24 hours a day, seven days a week; we can't live without it. Our bodies have the ability to heal themselves, shut down in a state of unconsciousness for several hours a day, and the process that happens after a human male sperm penetrates a female's egg is something truly amazing, some would say miraculous.

There are many miracles of life that happen each day, but we take them for granted, because we chalk it up to, that's just how life works. But what's interesting is the fact that many people look at these miracles of life and either believe in God, but struggle with their faith, or don't believe in God at all. Some people look at the gift of life as something that just happened (their birth), and they will just die and nothing happens to their soul; they're just dead.

What's amazing is that some people find it hard to believe in a higher power, but they don't find it hard to believe that the universe started from a grain of sand and then expanded into the enormous infinite universe of today. It's okay to question the idea of a higher power, because for me, the Big Bang theory generates questions that invariably lead back to the idea of a higher power.

If the Big Bang theory is correct, why did it occur? What was the force to make it happen—God? Why did the universe form the way it did, and why was Earth populated with life? What existed before the big bang? Was it God? If we came from nothingness, why is it hard to believe that when we die, our consciousness will live on separately from our bodies?

Imagine the reverse. Our souls are floating around earth, but not able to physically interact with the environment. It may seem impossible. We would then pray for physical bodies to allow us to interact with earth and all its treasures. Well, God has already given us that gift. We all have bodies that allow us to touch, smell, see, communicate, taste, feel and heal. It's a blessing, not a coincidence!

I wonder about all the things that had to happen 15-16 billion years ago to bring me into existence, then once in existence, I look back on all the things that were possible in my life. Do I believe in a higher power, do I believe in God? Yes, I do. And not because people say I should believe in God. I look at my life as proof, starting with my birth, then on to my near-death experience and beyond. Some people would say, what makes your life special—but that's just it—we're all special. It's a blessing just to be born. As I said, just imagine all of the people who had to meet, be attracted to each other and have sex at the right time for each one of us to be born. It's possible that none of us may have been born, but we were blessed to be able to come into existence and make our impact on the world and universe ... however small or big.

When I was young, my brother Jack told me that "with God, all things are possible." And that's what I believe. But I believe it not because he told me to; I believe it because that's what I've always felt in my soul. There are two facts of life that can't be denied—there is good and evil. In life, I tried to believe in good, love and God. How can you go wrong believing in these things? I believe in God, and with him, I know that all things are possible.

My life could have easily ended when I was hit by that car when I was four years old, but I was blessed with more time to make whatever positive impact I could in life. My near-death experience was my first peek into seeing that I was being watched over throughout life. That experience was the trigger for my spiritual journey with God.

Although the domestic violence I witnessed was the most horrific experience I had in life, I was blessed that I was able to get through that period, and more important, my mother made it through those times with her life. She was able to move on and have many joyous years on earth.

God has allowed me to give back and contribute to domestic violence shelters. While playing Santa Claus during the holidays, I've been able to bring smiles to the kids' faces at the domestic violence shelters. I've also played with the kids while their mothers attend counseling sessions at the shelters.

Growing up in the 'hood exposed me to gang violence, fights and drugs. At a young age, I had to fight my way to and from school. I've been jumped and beaten by several boys at once. I had to duck for cover when the gangs started shooting in the neighborhood, but I survived. God was watching over me.

Benny and I both started smoking weed in third grade—we were only eight years old. I remember being in class high as a kite. By the time we reached middle school, we were getting high pretty frequently and eventually, many of the guys who were getting high in the neighborhood were getting locked up, or killed. Benny jumped into the fast lane and started trying harder drugs, but I discovered basketball and was able to escape the path that many cats took. God utilized basketball as a vehicle to not only give me a life, but saved my life.

In 9th grade, I started going to the G-Town Y every day to play basketball. That was the best thing I could have done. I was able to get away from the kids in the neighborhood and eventually stopped weed. Each day, I got better and better at playing basketball—it really did save my life. I started hitting the books, including the Bible. I felt the spirit of God giving me the power to succeed and make all things possible.

For tenth grade, God guided me to Northeast High. Northeast pretty much had its basketball team set, but lucky for me the team still had tryouts. When all odds were against me, I made the JV team, and then the varsity team the following year. At my very last high school basketball game, it just so happens that the coach from Widener was scouting our star player. But he contacted my coach and recruited me for his college basketball program. With God, all things are possible.

God guided me to the right place again. It just so happens, that some of the Sixers came to Widener for pickup games and scrimmages prior to the start of their 1981-82 basketball season. Four years prior, I was the last pick when kids chose basketball teams for the neighborhood pickup games and now I was playing with NBA players. Guys who were my heroes, guys I dreamed about playing with, but it became a reality. With God ALL thing are possible.

I have to stress that the power of prayer played a major role in my life. It appeared that everything I prayed for was coming true for me. After my sophomore year in college, I prayed so hard to meet my soul mate—a girlfriend I could get serious with. Up to that point, I never really had a serious relationship. I was very picky. If I hooked up with a girl, she had to be special and had to have features I was attracted to.

God answered my prayers once again. I met Elle the very first day of my junior semester. I knew she was the right one for me. We clicked immediately. She had all the qualities I was looking for and more. With God, all things are possible.

At Widener, there wasn't a Kappa chapter. But I prayed to become a Kappa. The following year after I graduated college, I became a Kappa. It seems like when all odds were against me, God would turn the odds in my favor. Looking back, it was amazing all the blessings I received by the age of 23 years old.

Unfortunately, the friends I grew up with in the neighborhood were falling by the wayside. Drugs were taking their toll on them and it was sad to see my friends walking around with dirty buckets trying to make a few dollars washing cars in order to purchase some crack. I was so fortunate that I didn't go down the same path. I could have easily been strung out on crack as well, but I accepted God into my life and prayed for a better life. Benny tried boxing and I thought that would help him to escape the drug life, but he still stayed in that fast lane of money, women and drugs. Nothing wrong with women and money, but drugs can kill you.

During the time I was achieving my goals in life, Benny and I lost touch. We were now a part of two different worlds. But several years later, I ran into him while I was a finance manager at a drug and mental health facility. As I walked into the lobby, I saw him sitting in a chair and I was shocked. He looked horrible. He had major hair loss in certain spots ... and teeth missing; he was a shell of his younger pretty boy image. But Benny always had an animated personality and the gift of gab, which made him a likeable fellow, and that was the only good trait he still had left.

Benny lifted his head and saw me as I entered the lobby. He was shocked to see me, but still exhibited his animated personality.

"Hey Joey, what's up? What are you doing here?"

"I work here. My office is upstairs. I'm the finance manager."

"Aw, that's great. Glad to see you doing well."

I didn't dare ask him why he was there. It was pretty obvious. We chatted for a while, but I was saddened to see the state he was in.

"Hey look man, it was nice catching up with you, but I have to get back to work. Stay strong!"

"Okay Joey, take care man." On my way back to my office, I thought about how Benny had it all—great parents who made a nice living as a lawyer and a teacher; his parents owned a motel in Wildwood and had a nice house built in Mt. Airy. Benny used to be a pretty boy who had pretty girls all over him. When I was ten, I wished I were him, because he had everything I didn't. But now the roles were reversed. I was blessed with a great life and Benny was falling by the wayside due to drugs.

James Adams

In 1990, Elle and I were married. I was 27 and always thought I'd wait until 30 to get married, but not only did I love Elle and know she was my soul mate, I dreamed and prayed about having kids. After Elle and I were married, we tried right away to have kids, but we had no success for several years. After seeing specialists and having a few minor surgeries, we were blessed with a daughter, Christy, after four years of trying to conceive. We then tried for a second child and I prayed for a boy. Seven years later, God blessed us with a baby boy, Joseph. I now had Elle and two beautiful kids in my life. The odds seemed against us, but with God, all things are possible.

What made this time even more special is that we gave our kids a blessing that I didn't have—a household with both their father and mother in it. As I mentioned previously, I grew up without my father living in my household and vowed that I wouldn't allow that to happen to my kids. I wanted to be in my kids' life—see their first steps, be there for their first everything. Growing up, I would watch some TV shows and see the classic scene with the father, wife and kids sitting down to a nice family dinner. To be able to have a family dinner with my wife and kids is truly a blessing. It may seem like a small thing, but when you grow up without a father in your life, it can be a big thing, because it's something you see other people experience as a normal way of life and you start wishing you could have that experience

As life went on, I prayed many times and received many blessings. Elle and I had great jobs and were able to send our kids to private school and buy everything we "needed." The kids were growing nicely. Elle and I both completed our master's degrees. We were truly blessed.

But I often worried about my friend Benny and wondered how he was doing. As I said before, for me, Benny represented the road not taken in life. I didn't go down that path of drugs and fast living. Basketball saved my life. If it weren't for basketball, I wouldn't have gone to Widener, met Elle and had the family I have now. Without basketball, I may have gone down the same path of drugs and possibly fallen by the wayside. God made it all possible—He guided me on the right path.

One day, I ran into Ken at a gas station. Ken was Benny's cousin and used to hang out with Benny and me when we were young.

"Hey Joey, long time no see."

"Yeah, it's been a while," I said. "What's been up with everyone?"

Ken's face changed to a somber look. "You know Benny died, right?"

"No, I didn't. What happened?" I said, surprised, but I knew the answer.

"Those drugs caught up to him."

"That's a damn shame," I said. After catching up a little, Ken went on his way. Tears ran down my cheeks as I reflected back on the time when Benny and I were 10-year-olds crabbing down in Wildwood. We had our innocence and not a care in the world. It was all about fun back then. We had our whole lives ahead of us. At that time, we had the option of several paths to take in life. Unfortunately for my dear friend, my blood brother, he took the wrong one. Benny died a young man.

I often pray for Benny's soul and pray he's in heaven. Because looking at my life as proof, the one thing I know without a doubt is that with God, ALL things are possible.

THE END.

About the Author

James Adams, born in Philadelphia, Pennsylvania, is an Associate Controller at a University outside Philadelphia. He holds a B. S. degree from Widener University, a Master of Arts in Humanities degree from Arcadia University and is completing a Master of Business Administration degree at Utica College, NY. He lives in Philadelphia, Pennsylvania with his wife Lena, his daughter Christin, and his son James.

www.ingramcontent.com/pod-product-compliance
Lightning Source LLC
Chambersburg PA
CBHW031424290426
44110CB00011B/513